Student Book

New International Edition

Grade 6

Tara Lievesley, Deborah Herridge
Series editor: John Stringer

ALWAYS LEARNING

PEARSON

Pearson Education Limited is a company incorporated in England and Wales having its registered office at Edinburgh Gate, Harlow, Essex, CM20 2JE.

Registered company number: 872828

www.pearsonglobalschools.com

Text © Pearson Education Limited 2012
First published 2003. This edition published 2012.

20 19 18 17 16 15
IMP 10 9 8 7 6 5 4

British Library Cataloguing in Publication Data
A catalogue record for this book is available from the British Library

ISBN 978 0 435 13361 0

Edited by Glenys Davis
Designed by Scout Design Associates
Original illustrations © Pearson Education Limited, 2003, 2009, 2012
Illustrated by Rosie Brooks, Beehive Illustration Ltd
Picture research by Iman Naciri
Cover photo/illustration © Alamy Images
Indexed by Indexing Specialists (UK) Ltd
Printed and bound in Malaysia, CTP-PJB

Acknowledgements

The publisher would like to thank the following for their kind permission to reproduce their photographs:

(Key: b-bottom; c-centre; l-left; r-right; t-top)

Alamy Images: 2bl, 12tr, 15tr, 16tr, 16cl, 23bl, 30bl, 33b, 34br, 51tr, 52tr, 53tr, 64tr, 65tr, 68br, 75cl, 79cr, 91tr; **Corbis:** 44cr, 96c; **Dreamstime.com:** 42bl; **Fotolia.com:** 1cl, 3bl, 10bl, 11bl, 38tr, 38bl, 39tr, 62cl, 67br, 84bl, 88c; **Getty Images:** 80br; **Glow Images:** 2tr, 8r, 9t, 18cr, 24tr, 24bl, 26cr, 45b, 55br, 69tr; **Mary Evans Picture Library:** 19br; **Rex Features:** 22bl, 94bl; **Science Photo Library Ltd:** 22tr, 44tr, 45cr; **Shutterstock.com:** 7t, 8l, 10tr, 12bl, 14l, 14br, 15cl, 16bl, 17tl, 21br, 30tr, 32b, 36l, 40cr, 56cr, 57cr, 61cr, 66tr, 66cr, 74br, 75t, 84tr, 85tr, 86tr, 93br, 95bl; TopFoto: 87tr

All other images © Pearson Education

Every effort has been made to trace the copyright holders and we apologise in advance for any unintentional omissions. We would be pleased to insert the appropriate acknowledgement in any subsequent edition of this publication.

Contents

How to use this book

At the beginning of each Unit there are lists of things you should already know or be able to do.

This shows words in the Unit that are important. Learn and use them.

This box tells you what the lesson is about.

Find out what coloured words in bold mean in the Glossary at the back of the book.

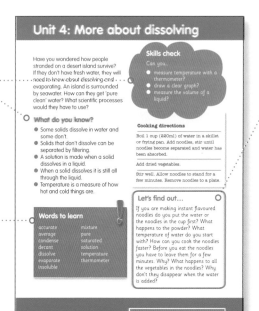

Think about these questions. By the end of the Unit you will know how to answer them.

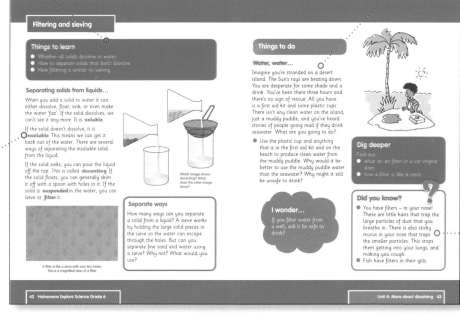

Try these activities. Your teacher will help you.

These boxes give you some fascinating facts.

This box tells you what you will find out during the lesson. Your teacher will help you.

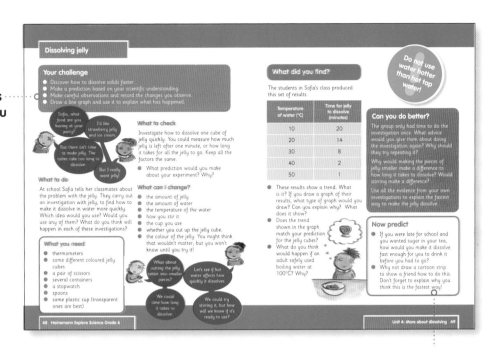

Use what you have learned to answer these questions.

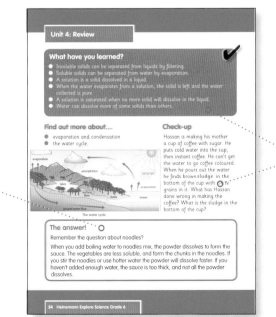

Here you find answers to important questions.

Check what you have learned.

Unit 1: Interdependence and adaptation

There is a rhyme about an old lady, who ate some strange things. First she swallowed a fly. Then she swallowed a spider, which she hoped would eat the fly. The spider wriggled. So she ate another animal to eat the spider. Which animal do you think she ate? Why is this like a food chain?

What do you know?

- What plants need to grow well.
- What animals need to grow and be healthy.
- Where different animals and plants are found.
- How animals and plants are suited to their environment.

Words to learn

adapted	pollution
consumer	predator
environment	prey
food chain	producer
fossil fuel	reduce, reuse, recycle
key	species
organism	suited
plant food	

Skills check

Can you...

- measure carefully?
- decide on the best way to present your results?
- use your science background knowledge to explain your ideas?
- explain why you think the way that you do?
- use a range of resources to find information, e.g. books and the Internet?
- use your debating skills?

Let's find out...

Farmers want plants to grow well. They give the plants nutrients, called fertilizers. When it rains, some fertilizer gets washed away into rivers and streams. Is this a problem for the animals that live there? Would any animals benefit? How?

Farmers put **pesticides** on their crops. What does a pesticide do? They also get washed into rivers and streams. Is this good or bad? Why?

Healthy plants

Things to learn

- How plants use light.
- Whether plants can grow without soil.
- How fertilizers are used.

Are you a good gardener?

Some people are called 'green-fingered'. This doesn't mean they have green coloured fingers. It means they are good at growing plants.

Each plant in these two pictures has something wrong with it. What could be wrong? What simple test could you do to find out? What equipment will you need? Make a list.

Bring me sunshine

Seeds do not need light to germinate. Plants need light to grow. Why does a growing plant need light?

Plants use light to make food. Scientists call this photosynthesis. 'Photo' means 'light' and 'synthesis' means 'to make'. They use their leaves to do this. Green plants make sugars from light energy, which they store as starch. It is used to make new leaves, roots, stems and flowers and seeds. Seeds are provided with their own food store. This is why a seed doesn't need light.

Things to do

Multi-vitamins and minerals for plants

A healthy human diet contains all the vitamins and minerals we need. Some humans take extra vitamins – especially if they are unwell.

Plants draw all the minerals they need from the soil. But some soils don't contain enough essential minerals. Plants don't grow well in them. They may not grow at all. Gardeners help plants to grow better with fertilizers. What do the plants get from these fertilizers?

- Look at the backs of packets and bottles of plant fertilizers. Make a table of the ingredients. Are all products the same? Are some better for some plants than others?

The leaf is the plant's food factory

I wonder...

Will a tomato grow as well with houseplant fertilizer?

Dig deeper

Find out:
- more about photosynthesis
- where photosynthesis takes place.

Did you know?

- During photosynthesis plants produce oxygen. Animals breathe in oxygen. A tree gives off enough oxygen in one year to keep four people alive!
- If you mark a tree 1 m above the ground, your mark will always be 1 m above the ground, no matter how tall the tree. This is because all plants grow from their tips, not from their root.

Feeding plants

Your challenge

- Discover whether a plant needs nutrients added to its diet.
- Make careful measurements.

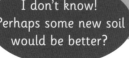

Are you feeling any better today?

Well, I've had plenty of water and sunlight, but I still feel weak

What you need is a tonic – something like tomato fertilizer

I don't know! Perhaps some new soil would be better?

What to do

Farmer Yousef has a problem with his tomato plants. Some are not growing as well as others. Yousef needs your help. What can you do? Scientists test or **trial** their ideas first. How could you test your idea? Do some trials with healthy plants. Here are some ideas.

What am I going to do with these tomato plants? They don't look healthy.

You could try giving them some fertilizer.

I could change the soil.

Would tomato fertilizer work best?

What other kinds could I try?

What you need

- tomato and houseplant fertilizer
- new compost/soil
- plant pots
- measuring cylinders
- a plastic pipette
- a tray of similar-sized tomato seedlings

What to check

Now try it yourselves.

- How will you know a plant has grown well? What observation or measurement will you make? Why does the plant have to be kept in the light and watered?
- What will you use as a **control**?

What did you find?

The students in the school Go for Green club decided to test all the suggestions to improve the health of the plants. They thought that measuring how tall each plant grew would be best.

Remedy	Amount plant grew in one week (cm)
no change (control)	3
tomato fertilizer	15
houseplant fertilizer	12
new soil	10
new soil and tomato fertilizer	14
new soil and houseplant fertilizer	12

- Which plant grew best? Did having new soil make a difference?
- What can you conclude? Which method would you use to help the sick plant? How does the evidence support your ideas?
- Draw a graph of your results. What kind of graph will you choose? Why?

Can you do better?

- How would you improve the accuracy of the investigation?
- Why could using a whole tray of plants be a good idea?

Now predict

- The local garden centre is running a competition for children to grow the biggest vegetable. Write down exactly what to do to make vegetables grow big. Explain carefully and clearly why you think your idea is the best. Use your learning so far.
- A scientist always tests ideas before sharing them. How would you present your evidence? Would a table be best? Or a graph, a bar chart or a series of pictures? Why should you report your investigation?

Identifying living things

Who are you?

We use keys to identify and name living things. Keys ask simple questions. Some have 'yes' or 'no' answers, e.g 'Has the animal got six legs?'. This is a branching key.

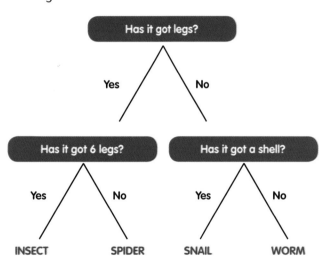

Some have questions with choices, e.g. 'How many legs has it got?'. The answers might be: 'four legs, go to question 3', 'six legs, go to question 4'. This is a go to key.

A consumer survey

A food chain shows what eats what, in a habitat.

Every food chain starts with a green plant. It is called a producer. It uses water, carbon dioxide from the air and light energy to manufacture or produce food. Can you remember what this food is called? This food provides the plant, and the animals that eat it, with energy. The plant uses the food to live and grow.

Animals are called consumers because they eat, or consume, these plants, or other animals. Some animals are called predators, because they eat other animals. The animals they eat are called prey.

The food that the plant produces passes up the food chain as energy from one animal to the next. The animal at the end of the food chain is called the 'top predator'.

I wonder...

Animals need to hunt or graze for their food. They need to be able to move around. But plants don't move around. Why not? How can they keep still and get the energy they need?

Things to do

Are you dependent?

All live and living things in a habitat are called organisms.

- Choose a habitat to explore. List all the organisms, both animals and plants, you find. Is there a plant that gives animals shelter? How might the plants depend on the animals? How do the animals depend on the plants?
- Sort the organisms you have identified into groups. Label groups as producers and consumers. Label which consumers are predators and which are prey. What do you notice about all the producers?

Dig deeper

Find out:
- what a food web is
- what an ecosystem is.

Did you know?

- The Amazon Rainforest alone produces enough oxygen for half the world's population.

Food chains

Things to learn
- How to construct a food chain for a particular habitat.
- How a collection of food chains are linked, by exploring a habitat.

Penguins are both predators and prey

A food chain in the sea

There are tiny plants that float in the sea. These are called plankton. They are eaten by small fish and a small shrimp called krill. The fish then are eaten by penguins and seals. Whales then eat the krill. Seals will eat penguins. So will some whales.

The relationship between these organisms is called a food chain. But writing it as a series of sentences is quite confusing.

The energy flows

Plankton is a green plant. It uses the energy from the Sun to make food. This energy is what the animals need from their food. These are food chains in the sea

Sun → green plankton → fish → penguin → seal

or

Sun → green plankton → krill → whale

When one animal eats another the energy moves up the food chain. We show this with an arrow. Each arrow shows the flow of energy. It points to the animal doing the eating.

Seals can be prey, too. They are often eaten by sharks

I wonder...

How do the tiny animals that live on coral reefs feed? And what can possibly eat them?

Sharks are top predators. They have no enemies – except humans...

Things to do

Draw a food chain

- Choose a different habitat from your last activity. List all the animals and plants you find.
- Put all the animals and plants that you have found in order of 'who eats who'. Draw arrows between the organisms. Show which way the food travels up the food chain. The arrow should start at the plant and point to the first consumer.
- Label the producer and the consumers. Label which consumers are predators and which are prey.
- Describe your food chain to someone else, without showing it to them. Can they draw it accurately?
- What is true of all the food chains your class has produced?

Dig deeper

Find out:
- more about how food chains work
- about food chains and you.
- if there are food chains that don't start with a green plant
- if any animals could use the energy from the Sun to make their own food.

Did you know?

- Some food chains at the bottom of the deepest seas start without the Sun. Bacteria harness the energy from chemicals, and these are eaten by other animals.
- Just by taking one animal or plant out of food chain, lots of other animals will be affected.

Plant producer

Make your own food

What do you do when you are hungry? You eat some food. The food gives you the energy to live. It helps you grow and maintain your body.

Imagine you told your teacher you were hungry. What if they told you to go and stand in the sunshine, and make your own food? It wouldn't work! But plants can do that. They make their own food using energy from sunlight.

Green plants are producers. They are the starting point of nearly every food chain.

Invisible gas and tasteless liquid

Green plants use the energy of the Sun to combine two materials to make a new one.

Carbon dioxide is an invisible, tasteless, odourless gas. It's all around us. We, and all other animals, produce it when we respire. It's a waste product of living and breathing.

Water, as you know, is odourless, tasteless and colourless. It's all around us, too.

Photosynthesis combines these two chemicals to make sugars. This amazing process takes place in the leaves of green plants. The leaves are the plant's food factory. From the sugars, the plants manufacture new materials for energy and for growth.

Things to do

Collecting sunlight

- Look up at a tall tree. Almost every bit of that tree was once carbon dioxide and water. The tree has combined them to make that huge trunk, the branches, leaves, roots, flowers and fruits. Only a tiny amount of mineral salts was drawn from the soil.

Teamwork

We produce carbon dioxide. We cannot live without oxygen. Plants need carbon dioxide for photosynthesis. They produce oxygen as a waste product. That's teamwork!

It's not quite as simple as that. Plants also need oxygen to respire and stay alive. But they produce far more oxygen then they use.

Dig deeper

Find out:
- what happens at night? Plants (and animals) go on respiring, but what happens to photosynthesis?

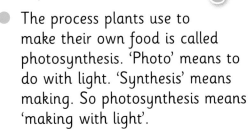

Did you know?

- The process plants use to make their own food is called photosynthesis. 'Photo' means to do with light. 'Synthesis' means making. So photosynthesis means 'making with light'.
- A waste product of photosynthesis is oxygen.

Life in the soil

Is it all mud?

Sometimes soil is called mud. We imagine mud as wet and brown. Not all soil is like this. Sandy soil is found in the desert. It is yellow coloured and dry. Soil rich in nutrients is found by rivers. This is more like mud. Where would a farmer grow his crops? Why?

Too wet or too dry

The Indian Grey Mongoose lives in burrows that it digs in the soil. They have long claws for this. They live in sandy and rocky places, like deserts. If they lived in wet soil they couldn't dig.

Earthworms live in soil. They eat rotting vegetation and soil. They help mix the soil as they move through it. They need soil to be moist so they can move. As they move through the soil and pass their waste, they supply the soil with nutrients.

Desert soil

Moles feed on earthworms in the soil

Scavenger plants

When animals and plants die, their bodies decay. This provides nutrients to the soil.

Some places in the world have very poor soil. Plants will germinate and flower next to a dead animal to get the nutrients it provides.

Remember to wash your hands carefully after handling soil

Things to do

Making a key

Do you remember what the two types of key are?

- Which key would you use to identify different soils?
- Collect some different soils. Feel them. Smell them. Look at them closely. What would be in your key questions?
- Which type of key would you use to identify animals that live in different soils? Could you use the same type for plants? Try it.

Dig deeper

Find out:
- how scientists group living things
- the names of the major groups of living things.

Did you know?

- You can use a branching key to identify anything, as long as you can ask simple yes/no questions.

Go to key

Q1 How wet is the soil?
Very   go to Q2;
a bit   go to Q3;
very dry   sandy soil

Q2 What colour is the soil?
red   go to Q4;
brown   go to Q5;

Q3 How big are the bits in the soil?
Big   rocky;
Small   go to Q4.

Continue this until you get to the end and have identified everything.

This is the start of a 'go to' key

I wonder...

There are plants found in almost every type of soil. Why do some plants that grow in poor soil trap and digest flies?

Things to learn
- Where different plants and animals are found.
- How plants and animals are suited to their own habitat.

How plants survive

Plants adapt to survive. They can grow anywhere. Some have adapted to grow in very cold places like the Arctic. Some live in very hot, humid places such as tropical rainforests.

These plants have adapted to live in a rain forest by growing very tall

In a rain forest there are plants at different heights. The plants near the ground don't get much sunlight. Some of them feed on other plants. They are called parasites. They have adapted to live like this. The tallest trees are called emergent plants. They can be over 60 m tall. They get lots of light. Other plants climb the trees to reach the Sun.

All these plants have adapted to suit their habitat.

Now you see me, now you don't

Animals adapt to their habitats. They have coats of fur or feathers that match their surroundings. A prey bird or animal will use this to hide from its predator. It makes them harder to find. This is called camouflage.

Some predators have coats to match their surrounding too. Why is this?

This ptarmigan white in winter

Things to do

Different places for different animals

You will see different animals in different places. Will you find a starfish in the desert? What about a gerbil in a pond? Does seaweed grow in the garden?

Certain animals are suited to living in water. Others are suited to living in dry conditions.

- Compare two different habitats, e.g. a rocky place and the seashore. List the plants and animals in each place. Do any live in both? If so, how are they different in each habitat? How are these living things adapted to their habitat?
- Invent a creature that is adapted to living in the habitat of your school classroom.

Global warming is causing glaciers to melt

I wonder...

The Earth is gradually warming up. We think this is because of people's actions. It could make the ice at the North and South Poles melt. What will happen to the world's sea level and to habitats?

Dig deeper

Find out:
- how organisms on the bottom of the ocean feed.
- how they are adapted to their habitat.

Did you know?

- The chameleon has the ultimate camouflage. It can change the colour of its entire body to match its surroundings.

Things to learn

- How humans have made an impact on the environment around them.
- Make decisions about whether the impact is good or bad.
- Research some of the changes that have happened to your environment.

Where have all the flowers gone?

Orchids are beautiful flowers. They grow in a variety of places. Some are very rare. The Dancing Girl orchid is one of these. It is found in the Himalayas. Scientists have been working to save it from dying out completely.

Madagascar has many rare orchids. They live in the rainforests. Humans are cutting down the trees and hunting the flowers for their beauty. They are losing their habitat. They are becoming extinct.

The Dancing Girls orchid

Where there were once small towns and villages, there are now large cities and lots more people. These pictures show New York 150 years ago and today

Step back in time

The world is changing. People make some of these changes. They make the place they live in suit them better. This may not suit the animals and plants that live there. The biggest changes have taken place in the last 200 years. For example, the first cars were invented in the late 1800s. Cars needed oil and petrol to work. Getting the oil out of the ground destroys habitats.

What other changes have people made to the environment that could destroy habitats?

A drawing of a Dodo, which is now extinct

Things to do

Where is the Dodo?

The Dodo was a large bird. It lived on the island of Mauritius. The Dodo had wings but didn't fly. It didn't need to. It had adapted to its habitat. It didn't have any predators until humans arrived on the island. Settlers from Holland brought other animals with them to Mauritius. Their dogs, ate the Dodo's eggs. There were fewer chicks born. The people cut down the trees where the Dodo lived. They wanted to grow crops, like tea and sugar cane. The Dodo's habitat was being destroyed. Then the Dodo was hunted for meat. As it couldn't fly away, it was an easy meal to catch. The dodo became extinct.

- Research and produce a timeline of the Dodo's extinction.
- Produce a presentation to explain what the settlers could have done to prevent the Dodo becoming extinct.

It's not all bad ...

Some people are now working to conserve plants and animals in the environment around them.

We think that the last wild Arabian Oryx was shot in 1972. It is not extinct though. Conservationists have bred some Oryx in zoos and released them into the wild again.

- What other animals have been saved from near extinction?

Dig deeper

Find out:
- about other species of plant that people have saved.
- about the first female African Nobel Prize winner Wangari Maathai and her work on conservation.

Did you know?

- The Botanical Gardens in Kew, London, are collecting seeds from all the plants in the world. They are making a seed bank. If a species of plant becomes endangered, they will use the seeds to grow more.

What a load of rubbish!

Things to learn

- The ways in which we can care more for the environment.
- How to reduce the amount of waste we produce.
- Why caring for the environment is important.

Reducing pollution

How can you help make less rubbish to go to the dump? Around the world, countries are following the idea of 'Reduce, Reuse, Recycle'. Have you heard people use this phrase? What does it mean?

When you reduce something, you try to make it smaller. Having less packaging around foods we buy, is reducing. Try buying a single large drinks container rather than lots of smaller ones. This produces less rubbish.

If you reuse something, you are finding a way to use it again. You can do this by filling up a container with water. This means you don't buy a new container. So you produce less rubbish.

One way of recycling is to give unwanted objects to other people. Or, if you make a model at school out of an old drinks container, you are recycling. You aren't throwing it away. You are producing less rubbish.

What other things can you reduce, reuse or recycle?

The rubbish dump

All the waste we produce has to go somewhere. It can make very large heaps and it is very slow to rot. It can also be very smelly.

Across the world people are trying to make less waste. In Abu Dhabi, each person produces about 2.3 kg of rubbish a day. The city is trying to reduce this to 1.5 kg per day. This is the same amount of rubbish produced by a person in Europe.

Rubbish can be an eyesore, but can also be a breeding ground for rats and foxes, which spread disease

How disgusting!

Pollution is when anything that isn't supposed to be in a place is put there. Even dropping litter or spitting out chewing gum onto the ground is polluting!

Things to do

Recycling in the classroom

- As a class, set up three different bins in your classroom. Label them 'paper', 'plastic' and 'cans'. Everyone should put their rubbish in the correct bin. Produce a poster to explain why the rubbish should be put in different bins.

Reusing in the classroom

- Use a range of old boxes, elastic bands, and plastic bottles to make an 'orchestra'. You can make guitars by stretching elastic bands over boxes. Shakers can be made from plastic bottles with dried beans or uncooked rice in them. Even old drinking glasses can make tunes if you put water in them, dip your finger in the water and run it around the rim.

Reducing in the classroom

- Keep a drawer of paper that has been used on one side. This can be used as scrap or rough paper. This reduces the amount of paper you need to use.

What other ways can you reduce, reuse and recycle?

Dig deeper

Find out:
- What can you make from old plastic bottles as part of recycling?
- Why did people years ago make less waste than we do now? How could we use this information?

Did you know?

- Reducing the amount of rubbish we make isn't the only way to help the environment. Reducing the amount of electricity and water we use is also important. Why?

I wonder...

What would happen to the environment if we didn't recycle?

Years ago, plastic bags weren't used. Why was this a good thing?

What have you learned?

- Green plants use sunlight to produce food so they can grow.
- Green plants are a source of food as they are at the start of almost every food chain.
- Food chains show the energy flow through living things in a habitat.
- Plants and animals are in a feeding relationship called a food chain.
- Animals and plants are adapted to their own habitat.
- Different animals and plants live in different habitats.
- Fertilizers are added to soils to provide plants with nutrients.
- You can use a key to identify plants and animals.
- Some ways in which we can 'go green' and care for the environment.
- How humans have changed their environment.
- How humans both destroy and protect living things around them.

Find out more about...

- Mei Ng and Vandana Shiva who worked on protecting the environment.
- how you can help look after your local habitats.

Check-up

The Go for Green Club are going to garden on a piece of waste ground in the school. They find it is full of rubbish, but they don't want to just throw it away. The soil is very sandy and the area has lots of trees hanging over it.

What should they do to make it a good place to grow plants?

The answer!

Do you remember the question about fertilizers and pesticides?

When fertilizers get into the rivers, they encourage the growth of river plants. This chokes the river so it can't flow properly. Fish depend on flowing water for food and oxygen. Without it they die.

A pesticide is a chemical that kills pests on the farmers' crops. If it gets into the river then it may kill organisms there as well.

Unit 2: Scientists

Science is the best way we have of finding out about the world. Science does not have the answer to everything. The exciting thing about science is that, at any moment, something may be discovered that changes the way we think about the world. And you might be the person to make that discovery...

What do you know?

- Scientists discover new things about the world and then explain them to others.
- Scientists come from all over the world; scientists are both women and men.
- You are learning to work as a scientist.

Skills check

Can you...

- plan good investigations?
- make predictions and explain why?
- collect evidence to test your ideas?
- make accurate observations and measurements?
- learn from the work of other scientists?
- use your imagination to draw conclusions and to make further predictions?
- explain how your evidence supports your prediction?

Words to learn

carbon dioxide   reflection
engineer   scientist

Let's find out...

'What puzzles me', said young Zach, 'is that my family always has stomach trouble after an aeroplane flight. The water we drink is always served from jugs, so there must be a water tank on the aeroplane. I wonder if the water is safe? Perhaps I should test some and see...'

Alhazen and how we see

Things to learn

- Science has a long history. Many people from different cultures have contributed.
- How combining observation with imagination has helped to explain what we experience every day.

How do we see?

Two thousand years ago, scientists like Ptolemy and Euclid believed that we saw because our eyes sent out magic rays. But they couldn't explain why these rays did not work in the dark. That's because there are no magic rays! A thousand years later, an Iraqi scientist explained how we saw. He didn't believe in magic rays. Abu Hasan Ibn al-Haitham or 'Alhazen' used observation, imagination and experiment to test his ideas. He wrote over two hundred books. These writings influenced European scientists, including Roger Bacon and Leonardo da Vinci.

This straw appears bent where it enters the water

Alhazen

How can I test my idea?

Alhazen tried some experiments with light. He worked inside a dark room with a hole in the wall. Outside, he hung lanterns. He found he could only see things in the room when the lantern light shone on them. 'So' he thought, 'the lantern light bounces off things and into my eye. My eye must collect this light, so that I can see'. This was good evidence. He was the first person to explain that the eye works as a collector — a receiver — of bounced or reflected light.

Things to do

Bend some light

Alhazen also explored how light was bent as it passed through water. He used these ideas to investigate how lenses magnify.

Explore the way that light is bent as it travels from air into water. Notice how a straw appears bent when you put it in a jar of water. Try dropping coins to cover a smaller coin on the bottom of a bucket of water – is the target really where it looks? Try looking at a picture through a jam jar filled with water. What happens to the picture?

with water. ■ Avoid contact with broken
doctor if skin irritation develops.
children. In case of accidental ingestion
e or contact a poison ontrol Center imm
Wet hands thoroughly with produ
it wiping. ■ For children under 6, u
sion. ■ Not recommended for infar

Water bends light. The print under this water drop is magnified

I wonder...
Why different animals see in different ways. Some insects can see ultraviolet light. Some snakes can see infrared light – they can see how hot things are.

Dig deeper
Find out:
- how the parts of your eye work
- how we see in three dimensions – binocular vision.

Did you know?
- 20/20 vision means that your eye can see what it should at a distance of 20 feet. Some people have 20/15 vision. They can see at 20 feet what most people can only see at 15!
- Modern 'super-reflectives' – like road signs and armbands – reflect a very large part of the light falling on them. They appear to shine with their own light.

Brunel and the railways

What can you learn from a picture?

Look carefully at this photograph. When this man was alive, Queen Victoria was queen of England. The man's waistcoat, wing collar, bow tie and tall 'stovepipe' hat are those of a wealthy Victorian. He has a pocket watch with a chain and fob, not a wristwatch. But all is not as it seems. Look closely. His trousers and boots are dirty. His clothes are stained with the mud of a shipyard. This is a practical, working man – an engineer. Behind him are the giant chains that will slow the huge ship he has designed, the *Great Eastern*, when it is launched.

Isambard Kingdom Brunel

The man in the photograph is Isambard Kingdom Brunel. He was born in 1806. His father was an engineer, and Isambard followed him into building ships, tunnels and railways. He nearly died, aged twenty, when his father's tunnel under London's River Thames collapsed. He was trapped under fallen timbers. But he survived. He went on to build the Great Western Railway, the three biggest steamships ever, and the Clifton suspension bridge near Bristol in the south-west of England. But he also invented a prefabricated hospital used in the Crimean War and a device to extract a coin stuck in his own throat.

Faster and faster

Isambard Kingdom Brunel hated wasting time. He wanted to go places fast. He built the Great Western Railway to speed up the journey between London and Bristol. London to Bristol is 118 miles or 190 km. Complete the table.

Date	Vehicle	Time	Km per hour
1784	Stagecoach	16 hours	
1837	Improved stagecoach	11 hours	
1851	First steam train	4.5 hours	
1912	Fast train		95
2003	Modern express	1.5 hours	

How train wheels stay on the track

You need:

- 3 m of wool or thin string
- 4 disposable cups
- 1 empty drinks can or card tube
- glue

Make your wheels

- Glue 2 of the cups, top to top. They are a tapering cone.
- Glue 2 cups bottom to bottom. They are a spreading cone.

Make your rails

Tie the string / wool to make a big loop. Put your hands into the string to make parallel lines or rails. Roll the wheels along the rails, by sloping the rails slightly.

Which wheels stay on the rails? Why?

Dig deeper

Find out:
- why wheels help make things move faster.

Did you know?

- Queen Victoria's husband was one of the first passengers on the Great Western Railway between London and Bath. Prince Albert travelled on the railway at the incredible speed of 44 mph – 'Not so fast next time, Mr Conductor,' he said.

Things to learn

- How scientists use their careful observations and measurements.
- How scientists use their imagination to question and explain the evidence they collect.

Mpemba and the ice cream

Mpemba was a thirteen-year-old school student in Tanzania who made his own ice cream. As he made it, he noticed that hot water froze faster than cold. He wondered why.

The answer challenged scientists. They suggest several theories. Ice forms on the top of cold water, but not on hot. Is ice insulating the cold water so it freezes more slowly? Warm water evaporates faster than cold — maybe some hot water evaporates so there is less water to freeze. Heating drives out gases like oxygen and carbon dioxide from water. Pure water without gases like these in it freezes faster, too. Mpemba decided to investigate.

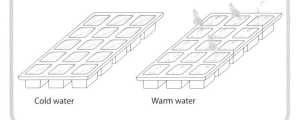

Cold water   Warm water

Einstein and the speed of light

How do you imagine Albert Einstein? Maybe you think of a wise old man with wild white hair much as he is in the picture. But when he made his greatest discoveries Einstein was young. He was strong and had thick dark hair.

When he was at school he asked difficult questions. His mother encouraged him to do this every day. She would say 'Albert, did you ask a good question at school today?'

At fourteen, he asked a very good question: 'What would the world look life if I rode on a ray of light?' This was a hard question to ask, because it needed imagination. It was even harder to answer. As you can't actually ride on a light ray you have to imagine the answer too!

Things to do

How fast does it freeze?

If you have a freezer, you can repeat Mpemba's investigation. You will need two ice trays and exactly the same amount of warm and cold water. You will need to start freezing both trays at the same time, in the same freezer. How will you tell which is freezing faster? How often will you check? What will you look for to decide which ideas might be the right explanation? Does it work with water and with ice cream?

The speed of light

Einstein imagined what it would be like to travel at the speed of light. Try it. Imagine you are sitting on a ray of light. At exactly twelve o'clock, you shoot away at 186 000 miles per second; but every time you look back at the clock, it is still twelve o'clock. At the speed of light, things change. Horizontal distances get shorter, and things you pass seem more crowded together. People look thin and tall. Tops of buildings seem to bend inwards and forwards. And colours begin to change. You appear blue to people you travel towards. As you whizz away, you seem red. Draw a 'speed of light' picture!

I wonder...

Can you think of a new question, then find a way of answering it?

Dig deeper

Find out:
- what happens to water when it freezes
- why adding salt to ice makes it freeze at a lower temperature.

Did you know?

- Einstein imagined that gravity could bend light. Stars have a strong gravity field around them. So he predicted that light rays would bend as they passed huge stars. He was proved right by evidence collected during an eclipse of the Sun in 1919, and his fame spread around the world.
- The face of the Jedi Master Yoda, in the Star Wars films, is based on Einstein, because of his apparent wisdom and understanding.

What have you learned?

- Scientists are people who make careful observations and measurements.
- Scientists are people who use their imagination to question and explain the evidence they collect.
- Scientists discover new things about the world.
- Scientists come from all over the world; scientists are both women and men.
- Science has a long history. Many people from different cultures have contributed.
- Some scientists are engineers – they apply science to make our lives better.
- Engineers imagine things which did not exist before.
- Engineers use the discoveries of science to create something new.
- You are learning to work as a scientist.

Find out more about...

- some other local or international scientists
- how they made their discoveries
- how people use science in everyday life.

Check-up

There are many questions that still puzzle scientists. We don't know what the universe is made of, how life began, what causes gravity or why we need to sleep. Maybe you can imagine some answers to difficult questions like these. But how will you test them?

The answer!

Remember that Zach had observed that he and his family had stomach trouble after long flights? Zach noticed that water in the aeroplane was served from jugs, and so must have come from a tank somewhere.

Zach collected water samples from the next nine flights, and tested them at home. He described what grew from the water as 'smelling like rotten peanut butter'. Seven samples contained harmful bacteria. One contained insect eggs.

His mother began advising other passengers not to drink airline water. Nowadays, when you fly, you will be given bottled water.

Unit 3: Humans

Your body is not just a big bag of food and blood! There are separate organs in it. You know some – the stomach, heart, lungs and brain. But there are others. All have at least one important job to do. All are vital to your health.

What do you know?

- You can name parts of your body.
- You can describe what some of these parts of the body are for and do.
- Humans need to eat a balanced diet to grow and be healthy.
- Your heart beats faster and you breathe more often and more deeply when you exercise.

Words to learn

abdomen	intestine
alveolus	oesophagus
anus	pulse
balanced diet	respiration
breathing	stomach
diaphragm	teeth
function	trachea
gut	

Skills check

Can you...

- make careful observations and measurements?
- collect evidence to test your ideas?
- describe how good your evidence is?
- realize when it is useful to use secondary sources?
- use your results to draw conclusions?

Let's find out...

'What I don't understand,' said Ahmed, 'is why my heart beats faster – and my lungs work harder – JUST when I need all my energy to run!'

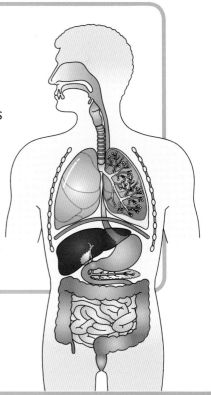

Where are your organs?

Things to learn

- Your body is made up of many different organs, with different jobs to do.
- These organs have scientific names.
- Where these organs are positioned in your body.

A lot of bits

Your body is about 60 per cent water. This water is mostly inside tiny packages called cells. There are more than fifty trillion cells in your body. They are organized into organs. There are big organs, like your liver. And there are small organs, like your eye or your ear.

A lot of jobs

Each of these organs has a special job, or function. Your eyes see, of course; and your ears hear. Your heart pumps blood. Some organs we might not think of as organs. Did you know that your skin is an organ? It is the largest organ in our body and protects all the other organs. It also gives us our appearance and shape. Imagine not having any skin!

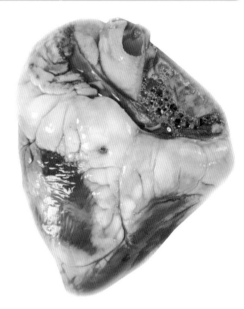

A human heart pumps blood around your body

Your stomach digests the food you eat. Your eyes see the food

What's its name?

Doctors have names for our organs. They are not always the names we use when talking to each other. Doctors will talk about our kidneys as part of our renal system. This comes from the Latin word 'renes', which means kidney. Many names for organs come from Latin. What others can you find?

Things to do

Where everything is

● Work in pairs. Lay a large sheet of paper on the floor. One of you lies on the paper. The other draws an outline round them. Then, together, draw where you think the organs are. Draw each one in a different colour and label it.

Organ	Similarly sized everyday object
heart	grapefruit
liver	A4 piece of paper
kidney	apple
intestines (uncoiled)	length of a football pitch

I wonder...

Why do you have an appendix? This little worm-shaped organ in your gut is nothing but trouble. Many people have had it removed.

How big is it all?

● Some organs are small. Some are big. Clench two fists. That's about the size of your heart. Cut a long triangle out of a sheet of A4 scrap paper. That's the size of your liver. Clench one fist. That's the size of one kidney. Using a picture to help you, draw your heart, lungs and two kidneys on scrap paper, cut them out and stick them in the right places on your outline.

Dig deeper

Find out:
● more about your body systems
● about water and waste.

Did you know?

● Your heart is not on the left of your body. It is in the middle. The left side is bigger than the right. So it seems to lean to your left.
● Your largest organ is your skin. The largest organ inside you is your liver. It is also the heaviest, weighing more than 1.5 kg.

Organization

Things to learn

- The function of some of your organs.
- How important your heart is.
- How organs work together.

Your circulatory system

heart

artery

vein

Systems

The organs of your body work together in systems. Each system has a scientific name and is made up of different organs. The circulatory system takes the blood around to every part of the body. It is made up of the pumping heart, the strong arteries that carry the blood away from it, the tiny capillaries, and the veins that carry the blood back.

The digestive system starts with your mouth, stomach and intestine. It breaks down your food to give you energy.

The respiratory system is made of the lungs and the airways that run to them. You use it when you breathe.

Systems work together

Organs work in systems, which work together. For example, when you exercise, you need energy. To get energy you need food and oxygen. Your digestive system breaks down your food. Your respiratory system provides oxygen to your body. The blood in your circulatory system carries both oxygen and food to your muscles, so that you can exercise.

Waste disposal

The job isn't over yet. There is the waste to take away. Waste products from food are carried back to the digestive system. Dead blood cells go there too. This passes out of the body and is flushed away. Waste gas — mostly carbon dioxide — is carried to your respiratory system. You breathe out more carbon dioxide than you breathe in.

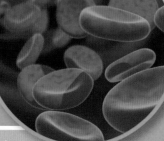

Red blood cells carrying oxygen to the muscles

Things to do

Heartbeat

Your heart beats steadily through your life – sometimes fast, sometimes slow. It will beat more than two million times in your lifetime. You can hear that beat. You need to shut out other noises, though.

A doctor uses a stethoscope to hear the heart going 'lub-dup, lub-dup.' But you can hear it by pushing a tube on the end of a plastic funnel. Hold the funnel to your chest. Put the end of the tube to your ear, and listen. Then find and count your pulse. Is it the same as your heart beat?

Dig deeper

Find out:
- what happens to your heart rate during exercise if you are very fit
- about heart disease
- what you blood is made of.

Did you know?

- There are ten organ systems in our bodies. Plants also have organ systems.

I wonder...

What happens if one of my organs stops working properly?

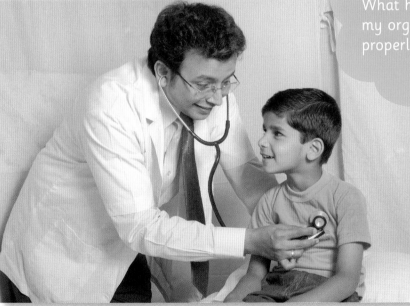

Why do you think the doctor listens to your heart from the back too?

Digestion

Things to learn

- The scientific names of the different organs in your body.
- The function of these organs.
- Why the digestive system is essential to all animals and how it works.

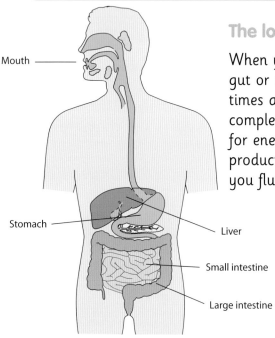

Mouth

Stomach

Liver

Small intestine

Large intestine

The long journey

When you swallow your food, it travels through your gut or digestive system. This is (mostly) a tube ten times as long as you are tall. On its way, food is completely changed. Nutrients – chemicals essential for energy, health and growth – are taken out. Waste products are added. It may be a day or more before you flush this body waste down the toilet.

Munching and mashing

To release nutrients, you need to break down your food. You cut, crush and squeeze it. Your teeth cut and chew. Then you swallow. Your food is squeezed down a tube called the oesophagus and into a muscular bag. This bag is your stomach; and it gets to work, squeezing and squashing, until your food is a liquid, which it squirts into your intestine.

Squirting and splashing

But that's not all. In your mouth and in your stomach, 17 special chemicals get to work, breaking down your food. Your stomach is about the same size as a large drink bottle. It takes two to four hours to turn your food into a thick soup. Then it is squirted into your small intestine. Its velvety lining acts like blotting paper, soaking up the useful food and passing a thick sludge into your large intestine.

You wouldn't recognise this meal once it is squirted out of your stomach!

Things to do

How long is your intestine?

You need a length of hosepipe. Or you could use a rope. It will need to be long! Just after the stomach is a special length of intestine called the duodenum. Chemicals are added here. The duodenum is 30 cm long. Next comes the small intestine – 6.5 m long. Finally, the large intestine – 1.8 m long. How much pipe will you need?

Now try to put it in a shoe box. Is it easy?

Moving food

Your body moves the food through your intestines by squeezing it. This is similar to when you squeeze toothpaste from a tube!

- Take a tube of toothpaste and gently squeeze from the bottom. What happens? Try squeezing from the middle. What happens now?
- Use a fabric tube, such as an old pair of tights. Put a tennis ball in the bottom. Using the squeezing of your hands behind the ball to move it to the top of the tights.

This is how your intestines work!

I wonder...

How much food will you eat in your lifetime?

All this tubing fits inside your body

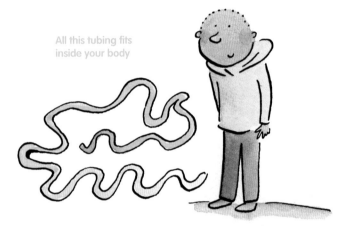

Dig deeper

Find out:
- what an enzyme is
- how enzymes help to digest your food.

Did you know?

- The muscles that make your food move through your intestine are strong enough to work even if you are upside down.

Breathing in and out

Things to learn

- Your body is made up of many different organs, with different functions.
- Why your respiratory system is essential.
- The scientific names of the different organs in your respiratory system.

You need oxygen

You need oxygen every minute of every day, even if you are sleeping. You can't store it. Without oxygen, you cannot release the energy from your food. You can take a deep breath and hold it for about a minute. But the carbon dioxide waste in your blood is sending a message to your brain: 'Breathe! Quick!'

These divers need to carry their own air to breathe under water

Special sponges

When you breathe in, air travels down a pipe called the trachea into your lungs. The journey doesn't stop there. The air then travels into smaller and smaller tubes. The smallest tubes have tiny bags at the end. These are called alveoli. Here the blood collects the oxygen and drops off carbon dioxide. Where does the blood go?

In and out

Your lungs have no muscles themselves to make them work. They work because they are in a sealed box – your chest. When your ribs are raised, your chest gets bigger. A strong muscle called the diaphragm moves down. This makes the space in your chest bigger. So your lungs get bigger and the air rushes into them. This is breathing in.

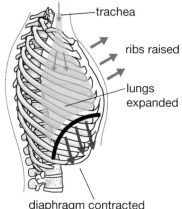

Breathing in

- trachea
- ribs raised
- lungs expanded
- diaphragm contracted and lowered

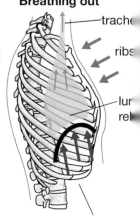

Breathing out

- trache
- ribs
- lur rel
- diaphragm relaxed and raised

Do you breathe through your nose?

Tear some tiny pieces of tissue paper. Put them on a piece of card. Hold your breath, and put the card, with the tissue on, horizontally between your nose and your mouth. Now breathe normally.

Does the paper stay where it is? You are a mouth-breather. Does it blow all over the place? You are a nose-breather.

Your nose contains hairs to stop dirt and some germs getting in. Why is it better to be a nose-breather?

What's in the air we breathe?

The air around us isn't only made of oxygen. This only makes up about 20 per cent of the air. The other gases in the air are shown in this table. Draw a chart to show the proportions of gases in the air. What type of chart would be best? A line graph, bar chart or pie chart?

Gas	Proportion in air
Nitrogen	78%
Oxgen	21%
Argon	1%
Carbon dioxide	0.04%
Helium and others	Traces only

There aren't just gases in the air. Ibn Sina, a Muslim physician in the 11th Century, recognised that some infectious diseases were carried in the air. He carefully observed how and when people got ill. What diseases do you know that are carried in the air? Make a list.

I wonder...

How can whales hold their breath for half an hour? Don't they need oxygen?

Dig deeper

Find out:
- how the air is changed when you breathe
- about asthma and how it is controlled.

Did you know?

- You need about three drink bottles full of air every minute. That's a room full every day. You will breathe 600 million times in your lifetime.

Things to learn

- Humans produce waste.
- Waste gases are lost through the lungs.
- Waste water and other materials are excreted by the kidneys.
- Your nervous system is your brain and nerves.
- our nervous system reacts to signals from your body, including your senses.
- Your nervous system controls what your body does.

Your kidneys

Another important system in your body deals with excretion. Excretion is getting rid of waste products. If you did not excrete waste, it would build up and harm your body. Your lungs excrete waste gases. Your kidneys excrete waste water.

Your kidneys are two organs, each about the size of your fist. They control the water in your body. They hold on to it if you are drying out, and get rid of it if you have too much.

Waste water or urine from the kidneys is stored in a bag called the bladder. It passes out of your body when you go to the lavatory. These waste products colour your urine pale yellow.

Filtering your blood

Your kidneys filter your blood. They let waste products through to your bladder. They hold back the precious salts that your body needs to stay healthy.

If your kidneys fail, you can use a special dialysis machine. A dialysis machine is an artificial kidney. You may be connected to it for an hour or more, three times a week. It filters your blood instead of your kidney.

Did you know?

- You can live with just one kidney. The other kidney will grow to do the work of two.
- People can sometimes give or donate one kidney to someone whose kidneys have failed.

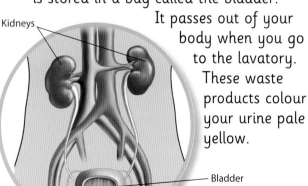

Kidneys

Bladder

Receiving signals

Your brain is about the size of a coconut. Its surface is wrinkled, like a walnut.

Your brain is in control of your body. Everything you see and hear, everything you smell and taste, is sent to your brain. It also gets signals from inside your body about all your other organs, and what they are doing.

Your brain could be overloaded. But it chooses the important signals, and ignores the unimportant ones.

Giving orders

Your brain deals with a lot of important business without bothering you. It keeps your heart beating. It speeds your heart up when you run. It keeps the food moving through your gut.

Sometimes, your brain alerts you to a problem. It tells you that you are hungry. It tells you that you need the lavatory. It tells you that you are tired.

Signals to and from the brain travel through special cells called neurons. These cells have long axons, which act like wires. Nerve cells are the longest cells in your body.

Everything you do, from breathing to laughing, is controlled by your brain.

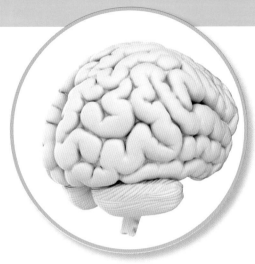

A model of the human brain

I wonder...

Why are your important sense organs on your head?

Did you know?

- A huge network of nerves brings messages to the brain. Signals zoom along them at 400 kph – four hundred kilometres an hour. That's about the speed of an airliner, or about 111 m a second.
- The biggest dinosaurs had a booster in the base of their tails to speed up the signals through their bodies.

What have you learned?

- Your body is made up of many different organs, with different jobs to do.
- These organs have special names and special places in your body.
- All these organs are very important to life. You could not live long without most of them.
- Your food is digested so that it can be taken to your cells, where its energy is released.
- Your heart pumps blood round your body, taking energy and oxygen to every cell.
- Your lungs exchange carbon dioxide for oxygen, which is essential for life.
- Your kidneys filter your blood.
- Your brain and nervous system control your body.

Find out more about...

- the different specialist cells that make up your body
- other body systems essential to life.

Check-up

You might have noticed that your head stays warm even when the rest of you is cold. Your brain is a high energy user. Explain why your body still needs oxygen and food, even when you are sitting perfectly still.

The answer!

Do you remember the question about why Ahmed's heart beat faster and he breathed deeper when he ran? Well, that brought more oxygen to his body. Without more oxygen to break down his food and give him more energy, he wouldn't be able to run at all!

Unit 4: More about dissolving

Have you wondered how people stranded on a desert island survive? If they don't have fresh water, they will need to know about dissolving and evaporating. An island is surrounded by seawater. How can they get 'pure clean' water? What scientific processes would they have to use?

What do you know?

- Some solids dissolve in water and some don't.
- Solids that don't dissolve can be separated by filtering.
- A solution is made when a solid dissolves in a liquid.
- When a solid dissolves it is still all through the liquid.
- Temperature is a measure of how hot and cold things are.

Words to learn

accurate	mixture
average	pure
condense	saturated
decant	solution
dissolve	temperature
evaporate	thermometer
insoluble	

Skills check

Can you...

- measure temperature with a thermometer?
- draw a clear graph?
- measure the volume of a liquid?

Cooking directions

Boil 1 cup (220ml) of water in a skillet or frying pan. Add noodles, stir until noodles become separated and water has been absorbed.

Add dried vegetables.

Stir well. Allow noodles to stand for a few minutes. Remove noodles to a plate.

Let's find out...

If you are making instant flavoured noodles do you put the water or the noodles in the cup first? What happens to the powder? What temperature of water do you start with? How can you cook the noodles faster? Before you eat the noodles you have to leave them for a few minutes. Why? What happens to all the vegetables in the noodles? Why don't they disappear when the water is added?

Filtering and sieving

Things to learn

- Whether all solids dissolve in water.
- How to separate solids that don't dissolve.
- How filtering is similar to sieving.

Separating solids from liquids...

When you add a solid to water it can either dissolve, float, sink, or even make the water 'fizz'. If the solid dissolves, we can't see it any more. It is **soluble**.

If the solid doesn't dissolve, it is **insoluble**. This means we can get it back out of the water. There are several ways of separating the insoluble solid from the liquid.

If the solid sinks, you can pour the liquid off the top. This is called **decanting**. If the solid floats, you can generally skim it off with a spoon with holes in it. If the solid is **suspended** in the water, you can sieve or **filter** it.

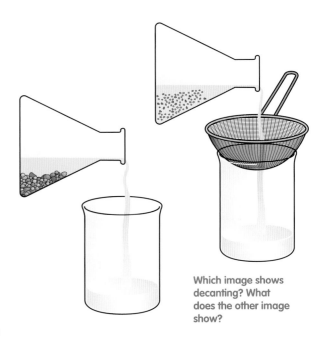

Which image shows decanting? What does the other image show?

A filter is like a sieve with very tiny holes. This is a magnified view of a filter

Separate ways

How many ways can you separate a solid from a liquid? A sieve works by holding the large solid pieces in the sieve so the water can escape through the holes. But can you separate fine sand and water using a sieve? Why not? What would you use?

Things to do

Water, water...

Imagine you're stranded on a desert island. The Sun's rays are beating down. You are desperate for some shade and a drink. You've been there three hours and there's no sign of rescue. All you have is a first aid kit and some plastic cups. There isn't any clean water on the island, just a muddy puddle, and you've heard stories of people going mad if they drink seawater. What are you going to do?

- Use the plastic cup and anything that is in the first aid kit and on the beach to produce clean water from the muddy puddle. Why would it be better to use the muddy puddle water than the seawater? Why might it still be unsafe to drink?

I wonder...

If you filter water from a well, will it be safe to drink?

Dig deeper

Find out:
- what an air filter in a car engine does
- how a filter is like a sieve.

Did you know?

- You have filters – in your nose! These are little hairs that trap the large particles of dust that you breathe in. There is also sticky mucus in your nose that traps the smaller particles. This stops them getting into your lungs, and making you cough.
- Fish have filters in their gills.

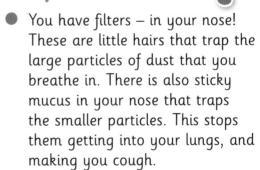

Separating solids and liquids

Things to learn

- What a solution is.
- Whether you can remove a solid from a solution by filtering.
- What happens to a solution when the water evaporates.

What's the answer?

Some solids disappear when you put them in water – this is a solution. The solids are soluble in water.

The solid hasn't really disappeared. It has dissolved. This means that it is still in the water, but the solid is in such small bits that it cannot be seen. You can sometimes tell the solid is still there. The water may be coloured, e.g. when you add powder paint. If the water is still transparent, you can taste the solid, e.g. sugar or salt.

Ink is a solution of coloured pigment in water

Which to remove?

How do you get the solid in a solution out again? Because the solid is dissolved in the liquid, it can't be sieved. The particles (or bits) of the solid are too mixed up and too small. Would filtering work?

To get the dissolved particles of solid back, you may need to remove the water. What do you know about making liquid water evaporate?

The study of solutions is part of science called chemistry. Jabir ibn Hayyan was an alchemist who was born in Persia (modern-day Iran) over 1200 years ago. He was the first to describe **crystallization**, which happens when you leave some some solutions to evaporate. Try it and see.

When something evaporates, the water escapes an leaves the solid residue behind

Things to do

Going, going, gone

If you leave a solution in a warm place the water will evaporate leaving the dissolved solid in the bottom of the dish. This is called the residue because it resides or stays behind. Instead of removing the solid from the liquid you are removing the water from the solid.

● Place some different solutions in dishes in a warm place. Think about how you can be scientific about this experiment. You should keep the experiment fair. How will you do this? Explain what happens and where the liquid goes.

When seawater evaporates, it leaves salt behind.
The white on the ground is salt from the sea

Dig deeper

Find out:
● more about how to separate a dissolved solid from the liquid it is dissolved in
● what the difference is between a solute and a solvent
● more about Jabir ibn Hayyan.

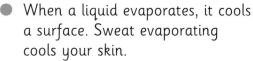

Did you know?

● When a liquid evaporates, it cools a surface. Sweat evaporating cools your skin.
● When you put nail varnish on it is wet. If you leave it for a couple of minutes it dries. This is because the solvent containing the varnish evaporates, leaving a hard, shiny layer on your nails.

I wonder...

Is evaporation the best way to separate rice from water? Explain what you would do.

Making water pure

Things to learn

- How to make water pure.
- What happens when water evaporates from a solution.

Where does it go?

If you want to recover a solid that was dissolved in water, then you leave the solution in a warm place. The water evaporates, leaving the solid behind. But where does the water go? Does some solid leave the dish with the water?

Solid particles are bigger than liquid particles. Solid particles are too heavy to escape the solution. Only liquid particles escape. The water will condense on a cold surface to form pure water.

You get pure water when you evaporate a salt solution. Do you get pure water if you do the same with inky water?

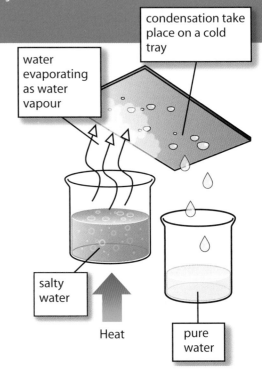

condensation take place on a cold tray

water evaporating as water vapour

salty water

Heat

pure water

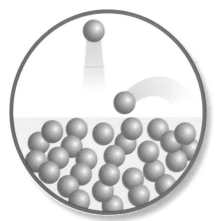

There are water particles escaping from the liquid surface
What is this process called?

Energy

If you eat more food, you gain energy. You can run around more. If you give a particle heat energy it will move faster. If a liquid particle moves fast enough it can escape the liquid. This is evaporation. Liquid particles that escape become vapour or gas.

Things to do

Should you drink seawater?

Remember your desert island? You cleaned the water from the puddle. You filtered it. But the puddle has now dried up in the sunshine. The water has evaporated. You are still thirsty, but the only water left is in the sea. This is too salty to drink. But you can't filter the salt out. How can you make the water drinkable?

When water evaporates from a solution, it doesn't disappear. It becomes water vapour. How can you collect the water vapour? You have two cups, a plastic bag and some salty water. Why not try putting the plastic bag over a cup of salt water? What do you think will happen?

- Test out other ways to collect the water vapour.
- Choose the way you think works best and draw it.

I wonder...

If you evaporate a soft drink, will you get pure water? What will be left in the bottom of the container?

Dig deeper

Find out:
- how you can speed up evaporation
- how evaporation and condensation make up the water cycle.

Did you know?

- Some air conditioning systems use evaporation. A fan blows over a wet surface. As the water evaporates, it cools the air. The fan blows the air into the room, cooling it down.
- The first woman alchemist was a Babylonian who lived over 4000 years ago. She used evaporation to make some of the first perfumes.

Dissolving jelly

Your challenge
- Discover how to dissolve solids faster.
- Make a prediction based on your scientific understanding.
- Make careful observations and record the changes you observe.
- Draw a line graph and use it to explain what has happened.

Sofia, what food are you having at your party?

I'd like strawberry jelly and ice cream.

But there isn't time to make jelly. The cubes take too long to dissolve.

But I really want jelly!

What to do

At school Safia tells her classmates about the problem with the jelly. They carry out an investigation with jelly, to find how to make it dissolve in water more quickly. Which idea would you use? Would you use any of them? What do you think will happen in each of these investigations?

What to check

Investigate how to dissolve one cube of jelly quickly. You could measure how much jelly is left after one minute, or how long it takes for all the jelly to go. Keep all the factors the same.

- What prediction would you make about your experiment? Why?

What can I change?
- the amount of jelly
- the amount of water
- the temperature of the water
- how you stir it
- the cup you use
- whether you cut up the jelly cube.
- the colour of the jelly. You might think that wouldn't matter; but you won't know until you try it!

What you need
- thermometers
- some different coloured jelly cubes
- a pair of scissors
- several containers
- a stopwatch
- spoons
- some plastic cup (transparent ones are best)

What about cutting the jelly tablet into smaller pieces?

Let's see if hot water affects how quickly it dissolves.

We could time how long it takes to dissolve.

We could try stirring it, but how will we know if it's ready to use?

What did you find?

The students in Sofia's class produced this set of results.

Temperature of water (°C)	Time for jelly to dissolve (minutes)
10	20
20	14
30	8
40	2
50	1

- These results show a trend. What is it? If you draw a graph of their results, what type of graph would you draw? Can you explain why? What does it show?
- Does the trend shown in the graph match your prediction for the jelly cubes?
- What do you think would happen if an adult safely used boiling water at 100°C? Why?

Do not use water hotter than hot tap water!

Can you do better?

The group only had time to do the investigation once. What advice would you give them about doing the investigation again? Why should they try repeating it?

Why would making the pieces of jelly smaller make a difference to how long it takes to dissolve? Would stirring make a difference?

Use all the evidence from your own investigations to explain the fastest way to make the jelly dissolve.

Now predict

- If you were late for school and you wanted sugar in your tea, how would you make it dissolve fast enough for you to drink it before you had to go?
- Why not draw a cartoon strip to show a friend how to do this. Don't forget to explain why you think this is the fastest way!

Dissolving sugar

Your challenge

- Discover how sweet you can make your tea.
- Make a scientific prediction about what you think will happen.
- Produce a line graph of results and use it to explain what is happening when you add the sugar to the tea.
- Explain why you need to repeat measurements.
- See if the evidence matches your prediction.

How many sugars do you have in your tea?

Just one, please.

I have twelve in my tea!

Don't you leave some sugar in the bottom of the cup?

It depends how much tea I have.

What to do

One of the students has a very sweet tooth. Will 12 teaspoons of sugar dissolve in one cup of tea? The students decide to test out their idea. They used sugar, a teaspoon and some warm water. They wanted to see when the sugar dissolved. They had a few ideas about what will happen and why. Which do you agree with? What do you predict?

The sugar will dissolve in the water until the water can't hold any more.

The more water you use the more sugar will dissolve.

What you need

- some sugar
- a measuring cylinder
- a teaspoon

When the water won't hold any more sugar, it will lie at the bottom of the cup.

What to check

Now try it yourselves.

- The students decided to stir the water as they added sugar. They kept adding sugar until they could see it on the bottom of the cup.
- What must be kept the same?

Maybe if you add the sugar slowly then the water can dissolve more.

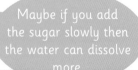

What did you find?

The students found out how many teaspoons of sugar dissolved in one cup of water. They then tried different sized cups. This was to see if their idea that if there is more water then more sugar can be dissolved in it was true.

- How did the students measure the volume of water?
- Here are the students' results. What kind of graph can be drawn from these results? Draw one for yourself. What pattern can you see in the graph?

Volume of water (ml)	Number of teaspoons of sugar
10	2
15	3
20	4
30	6
55	11

- Is there a limit to the number of teaspoons of sugar that water can hold?
- Does the evidence match your prediction?

Can you do better?

The students only used one kind of sugar. Could using different sugar make a difference?

Now predict

- If you had a cup that could hold 80 ml of water, how many teaspoons of sugar would you expect to dissolve? How does your experiment provide evidence for this? Use your line graph to help you.
- How would the temperature of the water make a difference to the results? (Hint: Look back at your jelly challenge.) To be scientific, write a short report to explain your ideas.

Mixing solids and liquids

Things to learn

- If there is a limit to how much solid a liquid will dissolve.
- Why water is special when we talk about solutions.
- Collect evidence and ideas including predictions.

Can't take any more

A piece of **saturated** fabric is holding as much water as it can. Your clothes might get saturated if you got caught in a rainstorm. But water can be saturated too. When a solid is added to water and dissolves, the solid particles fill the spaces between the liquid particles. Eventually the liquid particles have no space left to hold any more solid particles. No more will dissolve. This is called a 'saturated solution'.

If you have a full cup of tea and you add two teaspoons of sugar, what happens? Does the cup overflow? Try it. Explain what this shows about the sugar and the water particles. Use the diagram below to help you.

These are magnified crystals or grains

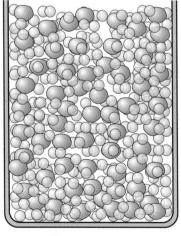

⬤ Solid Particle
◯ Water Particle

Does particle size matter?

Look at the size of particles or crystals of sugar and salt. Use a microscope. What do they look like? Look at some other substances that you know dissolve in water. Are the particle sizes all the same? Is there a link between particle size and how much will dissolve in water? What is it? Which do you think will dissolve first and why?

Things to do

That's the limit

Do some solids dissolve more than others? Is there a limit to how much each dissolves? For example, can the same volume of water dissolve two teaspoons of salt, or two teaspoons of sugar, or two teaspoons of cocoa powder?

- Plan an investigation to find the answer to this question. What will you have to keep the same to ensure a fair test?
- Carefully look at the particle size of your solids. Make a prediction. Don't forget to explain your ideas. You could draw pictures to help show your ideas.
- Decide how you will record your observations to share with others.
- Plan the investigation to get results that can be presented as a line graph.

The Plimsoll line shows how high the boat floats in the sea

Dig deeper

Find out:
- more about different types of solutions made with solids or liquids in water
- how a Plimsoll line is related to the salt dissolved in the sea.

Did you know?

- You can put oil and vinegar on a salad. This is called a dressing. Oil and vinegar don't mix. If you add mustard for flavour the oil and vinegar will mix. The mustard acts as a kind of glue.

What have you learned?

- Insoluble solids can be separated from liquids by filtering.
- Soluble solids can be separated from water by evaporation.
- A solution is a solid dissolved in a liquid.
- When the water evaporates from a solution, the solid is left and the water collected is pure.
- A solution is saturated when no more solid will dissolve in the liquid.
- Water can dissolve more of some solids than others.

Find out more about...

- evaporation and condensation
- the water cycle.

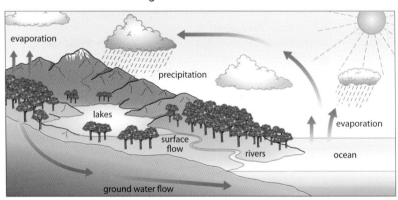

The water cycle

Check-up

Hassan is making his mother a cup of coffee with sugar. He puts cold water into the cup, then instant coffee. He can't get the water to go coffee coloured. When he pours out the water he finds brown **sludge** in the bottom of the cup with white grains in it. What has Hassan done wrong in making the coffee? What is the sludge in the bottom of the cup?

The answer!

Remember the question about noodles?

When you add boiling water to noodles mix, the powder dissolves to form the sauce. The vegetables are less soluble, and form the chunks in the noodles. If you stir the noodles or use hotter water the powder will dissolve faster. If you haven't added enough water, the sauce is too thick, and not all the powder dissolves.

Unit 5: Reversible and irreversible changes

We are surrounded by many different kinds of materials. Some, like rocks and wood, are natural. But many have been made for a particular task. To make a new material, other materials have to be changed. Some of these changes may be reversible – we can go back to where we started. But many are irreversible – a new material is formed. It may be nothing like the old ones!

What do you know?

- How to recognize evaporation, condensation, melting, freezing and dissolving.
- That evaporation, condensation, melting, freezing and dissolving are all reversible.
- That some changes aren't reversible.
- What happens when materials evaporate, condense, melt, freeze and dissolve.

Words to learn

chemical reaction
irreversible
reversible

Skills check

Can you ...

- make careful observations and measurements?
- collect evidence to test your ideas?
- see how good your evidence is?
- use your evidence to explain what you've found out?
- say how evidence supports your prediction.

Let's find out...

After a Diwali firework party, Hardip went round the garden. He collected all the fireworks he had watched the night before. 'I'm going to have another firework display tonight,' he told his mother. 'Not with those fireworks!' said his mother. 'Why not?' asked Hardip.

Evaporation

Things to learn

- What happens when solids are added to water.
- How to get an undissolved solid back from water.
- How to get a dissolved solid back from water.
- What happens to some materials as they are heated and cooled.
- Burning materials can be dangerous.

Sand and salt

'It's a disaster,' said Mrs Hamad. 'The bags have burst, and sand and salt are all mixed together.'

'Don't worry, Miss,' said Yunis. 'I know how to separate them.' 'How can you do that?' his teacher asked. 'All you need to know is that salt dissolves – and sand doesn't,' said Yunis.

Yunis used evaporation to get the salt back. He used filtration to get the sand back. But which did he do first – and why?

Chocolates

These chocolates were made in moulds. To make the shape of each chocolate, the chocolate is warmed. It becomes liquid and fills a mould. The cook leaves it to cool. The mould is taken away and the chocolate is left in its new shape. (Chocolate melts at the temperature of your mouth – which helps make it so tasty!)

Things to do

What happens with water?

When you add familiar foods to water, such as sugar to your tea, or salt to your soup, you expect them to dissolve. They seem to have disappeared – but you know by the taste that they are still there.

- But what about other safe materials? Does powder paint dissolve easily? Try adding water to **cornflour**, stirring all the time. Try some **indigestion powders** – like 'liver salts'. What happens?
- Finally, try **plaster of Paris** Something amazing happens! Not all materials need to be heated to speed up dissolving.

I wonder...

What is it that burns when we light a candle?

Fire

What's left after a fire? Some things aren't changed much. You might find nails in the ashes but what about wood? The ashes can't be used to make anything. The change is irreversible.

You can be changed by heat too, but not for the better! Skin can burn easily, so always be careful with fire. If you are ever burned, it is important to remove the heat. Quickly put your burnt fingers or arm under a cold water tap – and keep it there. Without the heat, your skin can recover.

Dig deeper

Find out:
- more about burning and the fire triangle.

Did you know?

- Cooking is the most common way to make irreversible changes. You can't get the eggs and flour back from a cake mixture!
- Rusting is an irreversible change.

Making new materials

Your challenge

- Explore what happens when different materials are mixed together.
- Decide whether the changes are reversible or not.
- Describe new materials that are made.
- Explain what happened, using what you know about science.

Sayyid was making a plaster of Paris model. 'This feels warm!' he said to his older brother. 'What did you do to it?' asked Tariq. 'Did you put it in the oven?' 'I didn't do anything to it," said Sayyid. 'I just mixed the white powder with water.'

Sayyid was puzzled. But Tariq told him that while lots of changes needed heat, some made heat. Maybe this was one of them. 'Try mixing these,' Tariq said, giving him some more kitchen materials. 'Don't worry – they're all safe!'

What to do

Mix together some of these:

- plaster of Paris and water
- liver salts and water
- bicarbonate of soda (or baking powder) and vinegar
- washing soda and lemon juice

What you need

- materials to mix
- water
- a measuring cylinder

What to check

Now try it yourselves.

- Use small amounts of these materials.
- Observe carefully what happens.
- Record what happens.
- Explain what happens using your scientific knowledge.

Things to do

Sayyid was surprised with his results. But he was too excited to complete the table properly. He's left some gaps.

● Copy and complete the table using your own test results.

Sayyid showed Tariq his results. 'These are all **chemical reactions**,' his brother told him. What did Tariq mean?

Now predict

● Sayyid melted butter. Then he melted syrup. He planned to make baklava. 'Are those irreversible reactions?' asked his big brother. Explain carefully the difference between a reversible change and an irreversible one, giving your reasons, so that Sayyid's big brother can understand it. How could you prove it with an experiment? You could demonstrate this to the rest of the class.

Solid to mix	Liquid to mix	What happened	Why I think it happened
plaster of Paris	water	It got warm! The plaster dried out and became hard. This is irreversible.	This is called a reaction. Some reactions need heat to get them going – but some produce heat.
liver salts		It bubbled and fizzed. The liquid was clear but the salts were still there.	The salts dissolved in the water. The reaction made a gas. The gas made the liquid bubble.
bicarbonate of soda	vinegar		The reaction made a gas. The gas made the bubbles.
washing soda	lemon juice	Lots of fizzing.	

Can you do better?

How good is your evidence? Use it to describe when an irreversible change takes place. What should you look for?

How do we use these reactions to help us in everyday life? When do builders, or cooks, or people with indigestion, use these new materials?

Can you get an irreversible change without mixing chemicals?

Let me saw your leg off and I'll tell you!

Irreversible change

Your challenge
- Find out what happens when different materials are burned.
- Discover what new materials are made.
- Recognize that some of these new materials cannot be seen.
- Take great care.

Where does the candle wax go, Dad?

I don't know. Maybe it just disappears?

What you need
- a burning candle, secured in a safe tray of sand
- a tin tray or can lid held in pliers or tongs
- a glass jar of ice

What to check
Try it yourselves.
- What do you think will happen?
- How will you test for the gases?
- Will you be able to name any?

Farah knew that couldn't be right.

'I think something new is made,' said Farah.

'But we can't see it.'

What to do

Farah puzzled about the disappearing candle. 'I think the candle must make a gas of some kind,' she thought. 'Only a gas could be invisible.'

What would you do to test this?

Suppose one of the gases was water. How can you tell that there is water in the air?

Maybe things just burn away to nothing.

That can't be right. When things burn, new things are made.

I think candles burn to give us a gas – or maybe some gases.

If we can't see them, how can we tell they are there?

Can you do better?

Farah held tiny pieces of different safe materials in the flame using the tongs. She was curious to see what was made when they were burned. Farah recorded her observations in a table. You could do the same.

⚠️ Take care when using flames

What did you find?

Farah watched as the candle burned down. Here are her observations.

The candle is white and cold. It is a solid. When we light it, the wick turns black. The solid candle becomes liquid near the wick. The flame is blue near the wick, then yellow further away. You can smell the burning.

We held a tin lid above the flame. It got smoky with soot. We think that might be from the wick. We held a cold glass jar above the flame. Water condensed on the jar. It dripped onto the candle. So one new material was water.

Our teacher told us that candles produce carbon dioxide gas, too.

- Was Farah correct in saying the candle makes a gas when it burns?
- How would you test for carbon dioxide?

Now predict

- When Farah cooked breakfast, she always burned the toast. What's the difference between heating things and burning things, she wondered? How could you explain this to your parents? Produce a checklist of things to look for so you can tell the difference.

What have you learned?

- How to dissolve and separate solids from water.
- What happens when something dissolves.
- What happens when something is heated.
- How to tell if a change is reversible or not.
- How to make careful observations.
- To recognize when new materials have been made.
- To explain how good your evidence is.
- To use your evidence to explain what you've found out.
- To say if your evidence supports your prediction.
- To work safely and carefully.

Find out more about...

- how new materials, like chemicals, are made in industry.

Check-up

Nadia and Zadie have a gas barbecue. 'It's great,' they said. 'The gas just seems to go on forever.' Why aren't they right? What is happening to the gas?

The answer!

Hardip couldn't reuse the fireworks as they had been burned and changed irreversibly. The materials in the fireworks had changed to gases. At least the burning gases had given Hardip a great firework display!

Unit 6: Forces in action

Did you know that forces are acting on you all the time? Whenever you do something you are exerting a force. When you take a step, you push against the ground. The ground is also pushing back at you.

What do you know?

- Forces are pushes and pulls.
- Forces act in particular directions.
- We can't see forces but we can measure them and observe what they do.
- Forces can make objects move, stop, change speed, direction or even shape.
- Friction is a force that slows things down.
- Lubrication reduces friction between solid surfaces.
- Air resistance is a force that slows things moving in air.
- Water resistance is a force that slows things moving in water.
- Streamlined shapes can reduce air and water resistance.

Words to learn

action	mass
balanced	newton
forcemeter	newtonmeter
gravity	reaction
Jupiter	unbalanced
kilogram	upthrust
matter	weight

Skills check

Can you...

- make careful observations and measurements?
- collect evidence to test your ideas?
- make predictions about your ideas?
- notice patterns in your results?
- explain what you've found out?
- decide if your evidence is good enough?
- say if your evidence supports your predictions?

Let's find out...

Farida went to the market. She bought eggs, fish and rice and put them into a plastic carrier bag. As she lifted the bag the handles snapped and the groceries fell all over the road. The fish and rice spilled out and the eggs broke. Explain why all this happened – as forces in action!

Weight and gravity

Things to learn

- How gravity acts on objects.
- How weight, mass, the force of gravity are related.
- What the units of forces are measured in.

Gravity pulls you back down to Earth again

Gravity

Gravity is a force of attraction that pulls objects together. Every object has this force. We are all attracted to each other and everything around us. For small objects, these are small forces of attraction.

The Earth's gravity pulls everything towards its centre. This keeps us on its surface. The Earth has a huge force of attraction. Without gravity, everything on the Earth would fly off into space, including the air we breathe.

How 'massive'?

The mass of an object is how much 'stuff' or matter, it is made up of. It is measured in kilogram (kg). The more matter an object has, the more mass it has.

The bigger an object's mass, the bigger its attractive force of gravity. The amount of gravity also depends on how close the object is. The closer the object, the bigger the force.

The Earth is a huge object. It has a huge mass. It has a huge gravitational force. We are very close to it, as we are standing on it. We are pulled down by its force.

Weight

The force of gravity attracts everything and gives things weight. Weight is measured in newtons (N). It is a force. Weight is the amount of mass an object has and the amount of gravity acting on it. An object with a small amount of mass has a small weight.

This box has more 'stuff' in it, so it has more mass than an empty box

Things to do

Measure a force

We measure forces in newtons. The symbol for a newton is N. One newton is about the force you need to pick up an average-sized apple. Ten newtons are roughly the force you would need to lift 1 kg.

A forcemeter measures an objects weight. Hook an object onto the spring. Gravity pulls down the object. The pull of gravity on the object stretches the spring. The force in newtons can be read on the scale.

- Try this yourself. Measure the weight in newtons of some objects using a forcemeter.
- Now find the mass of your objects by putting them on a balance. Remember, mass is a measure of how much matter something has. We measure mass in grams and kilograms. These are our everyday measures of mass. Can you find a connection between mass and weight?

This forcemeter will tell you how many newtons are needed to move this brick

Dig deeper

Find out:
- more about how weight can change
- why you couldn't stand up on the biggest planets.

Did you know?

- The Moon is smaller than the Earth. It has a smaller force of gravity. It is only one-sixth the size of the Earth so it has one-sixth of the gravity.
- If you could stand on Jupiter you'd weigh three times as much as you do on Earth. Jupiter's gravity is stronger than Earth's.

I wonder...

If you weigh more or less on top of a mountain?

Energy in movement

Things to learn
- We need energy to pull, throw, or drop something.
- Our energy can be forced into movement energy.

The magic bicycle

Aleysha had a new bicycle. She was frightened to ride it. She was afraid she might fall off. Her father stood her bicycle up and pushed it gently towards her. To her surprise, it stayed upright until she caught it. 'The bicycle will go on rolling until something slows it down and stops it,' said her father. Aleysha found that hard to believe.

Eating breakfast gives you the energy to ride a bicycle

Adding energy

Aleysha pushed her bicycle to the top of the hill. It was hard work. 'You've given your bicycle a lot of energy,' said her father. 'If you let it go now, you will be surprised how far it rolls!' The bicycle had been given energy. The energy is stored in it. When you let go of the bicycle it moves. The stored energy turns into movement energy.

Energy chain

You can't see energy, or touch it. But without energy nothing would happen. When Aleysha had her breakfast that morning, it gave her energy. She could ride her bicycle and push it to the top of the hill.

Things to do

Forces in motion

- Set up a ramp, using a plank of wood resting on a pile of books. Make a wall of building bricks just a little way from the foot of the plank. Put a toy car at the top of the plank. Will it knock down the wall? If it doesn't, how can you give it more energy so that it can?

When you move an object higher, you give it more 'stored' energy. Scientists call this energy potential energy. When you let go of the object, gravity pulls it downwards. This turns the potential energy into movement energy. If you make an object heavier, you can also give it energy. The more energy you put into the object the more it can move.

Dig deeper

Find out:
- how forces make things change direction
- what the scientific names of some forces are.

Did you know?

- When you kick a football, you give it energy. But once it is in the air, two other forces act on it. One is gravity, pulling it back to Earth. The other is air resistance, slowing it down. Without these two forces, the football would travel forever.

I wonder...

If you go bowling, why does a heavier ball knock down more pins?

Direction of forces

Things to learn

- Several forces may act on an object at the same time.
- Forces have size and direction.
- How we represent force size and direction to others.

Pair up

Forces don't act alone. When you use a force to push an object, the object pushes back at you. When you pull an object it pulls back at you.

When you pull a chair from under a table you use force to move it. You can also feel its force pulling back at you. The force you feel is its weight (in newtons). This is why it feels heavy.

Remember the link between matter, mass and weight? The bigger the chair, the greater the mass (in kg) it has. The greater the mass, the more gravity acts on it so the more weight it has.

The force you use is called the action. The opposite force you feel, is called the reaction. The action and reaction always act in opposite directions.

For every action, there is always a reaction, even if it is very small. Identify some actions and reactions in your movements.

Balancing act

When something is still we say that the forces acting on it are balanced. That means they are the same size or strength. They are said to be equal and opposite. It is like a tug of war with both sides pulling the same – nobody wins! As soon as one side pulls with more force than the other, the forces are unbalanced. That side wins.

Things to do

Drawing forces

Scientists use diagrams to communicate, such as circuit diagrams. We can draw diagrams of forces. These show the size and direction of the force. We draw these forces as arrows.

The length of the arrow shows how strong it is. A short arrow is a weak force. A long arrow is a strong force.

The way the arrow points shows the direction of the force. The arrow always points in the direction of movement, whether it's a pull or a push.

Dig deeper

Find out:
● about Sir Isaac Newton and his work on gravity.

Did you know?

● Helicopters, hawks or hornets can hover. The uplift force of their rotors or wings is exactly balanced by the downward pull of gravity.
● To escape the force of the Earth's gravity a rocket needs to accelerate quickly after its launch. The escape velocity is about 40 000 km per hour.

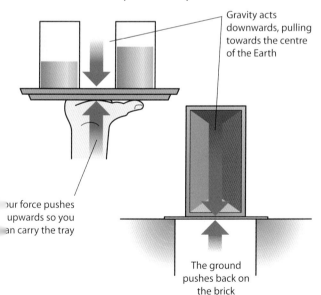

Gravity acts downwards, pulling towards the centre of the Earth

our force pushes upwards so you can carry the tray

The ground pushes back on the brick

● Draw the force arrows on the pictures on the worksheet.

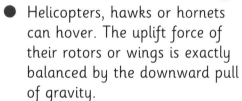

I wonder...

Why is it easier for two people to lift a heavy object than for one person to lift it on their own? Draw arrows on a diagram to show this.

Investigating upthrust

Your challenge
- Find out about the upward force water exerts on a submerged object.
- Make careful measurements of force using a forcemeter.
- Use tables to present results and identify patterns within them.
- Communicate these patterns scientifically.

Anya decided to find out why it was easier to exercise in water.

What to do

Anya measured the weight of some objects in newtons. Next she estimated what they would weigh in water. She put the objects in water and carefully read the value on her forcemeter.

She then did some simple maths:

Weight in air − **weight in water** = **push of the water**

She calculated the force of **upthrust** the water had.

What you need
- a forcemeter
- several objects that will sink in water and can be attached to the forcemeter
- a deep bowl of water
- paper towels

What to check

Now try it yourselves.

- How will you make sure that the object does not touch the bottom of the bowl?
- Repeat the measurement several times to be certain.

What did you find?

Anya put the results of her test into a table. She noticed that the objects always weighed less in water than in air.

She thought that the water was pushing up against the object and supporting some of its weight.

● Draw a table and graph of your results. Which set of measurements would you plot on the graph?

Object	Weight in air (N)	Weight in water (N)	Upthrust of Water (N)
staple gun	1.5	1	0.5
bunch of keys	2	0.85	0.15
scissors	0.75	0.55	0.2
rock	3.5	2.8	0.7
hole punch	1.3	0.9	0.4
bags of marbles	1.5	1.1	0.4

Can you do better?

If you did this investigation again is there anything you would change or do differently?

How good is your evidence?

Did your evidence support your prediction?

Now predict

● What do you think is happening to the mass of your objects when they are put into water? If an object had a mass of 200 g in air, what do you think its mass would be in water? How could you test this?
● Does gravity work through water? How do you know?

Stretching springs

Your challenge

- Find the relationship between stretching springs and the forces acting on it.
- Make careful measurements of length.
- Represent data in a line graph and use this to identify patterns in the data.

Mrs Malik's class is investigating what happens to a varity of springs when masses are suspended from them.

I think they will stretch the same amount with each mass.

They'll stretch lots to begin with. The stretch will get less as the masses get heavier.

They'll stop stretching eventually.

Do you agree with the students? What do you think will happen? Try it yourself.

What to do

Decide what measurement to make. Now add your masses one at a time and record how far the spring stretches.

What you need

- a secure hook or chair back to attach your spring to
- different springs
- hanging masses
- a metre rule
- paper and scissors to cut out paper springs.

What to check

Now try it yourselves.

- Decide where to measure from.
- Increase the mass by the same amount each time.
- Avoid snapping the paper spring.
- Does it matter what sort of spring you use?
- Record measurements in a table.

It might be easier if we measured from the table to the bottom of the mass.

Maybe we could mark the length on a piece card then measur later.

What did you find?

Mrs Malik's class all did the same investigation and used the same springs. They added 50 g weights one at a time. They measured the length of the spring each time. They put all of their results together and took a class average. Why do you think they did this?

Total mass added (g)	Length of spring (cm)	Length of stretch from resting position (cm)
0	15	0
50	19	4
100	23	8
150	25.5	10.5
200	27	12
250	28	13
300	28.5	13.5
350	29	14
400	29	14

The class used a spreadsheet to record their results. Drew a line graph using their data. They thought they noticed a pattern in the results.

- Can you see what the pattern is?
- Draw a graph of your results. Tell the story of your graph.
- Draw a force diagram with arrows to show what is happening in your experiment.

Can you do better?

Find out:
- If you did this investigation again would you do anything differently? Why?
- Can you write a general rule to explain what was happening?
- Could you use your graph to predict how far the spring stretches at weights you haven't tried yet?
- Would your rule apply to all types of spring?
- Would your rule work for other objects that stretch like a spring?

Now predict

- When people do a bungee jump, they throw themselves from a high place attached to a thick elastic cord. They bounce back before they hit the ground. Each person must be weighed before they jump. Why is this?

Air resistance

Things to learn

● How air resistance and friction are related.
● Which direction air resistance acts.
● How different objects areas are affected by air resistance.

Air friction

Friction is a force. It slows down moving objects. Friction may help them start moving in the first place. It is often called 'grip'. Friction happens when two surfaces rub together. The rougher the surfaces rubbing together, the greater the friction.

Air resistance is a special kind of friction. When an object moves, through the air, it rubs against air particles. The faster the object is moving, the greater the air resistance. This is because the object has to push the air particles out of the way faster.

A modern parachute

Leonardo's parachute

Leonardo da Vinci was an Italian scientist and inventor. He made the first parachute in about 1470. He made it out of wood and cloth. Adrian Nicholas tested a modern copy of this design in 2007.

When a parachute is opened, it slows the object or person attached to it. The parachutes size and shape affects the amount of air resistance. The bigger the parachute, the more air resistance they have.

Falling fast

An Italian scientist called Galileo believed that if you dropped two different objects from the same height they would hit the ground at the same time. When **astronauts** did this experiment on the Moon Galileo was proved right. There was no air on the Moon to resist the pull of its gravity, so a rock and a feather weren't slowed down as they fell. They hit the ground together.

Galileo

Things to do

Make a parachute

Make some different-sized parachutes out of tissue paper and thread. Use paperclips to represent a person. Drop your parachutes from the highest safe place you can (the top of a safe stairwell, for instance). Time their **descent** using a stopwatch. What must you do to keep your test fair? Which takes the longest to fall? Which is the fastest? Is it the shape that matters or the surface area? Can you think of some more parachute questions to investigate?

Can you see the air push against the parachure?

I wonder...

Why doesn't a pendulum keep swinging forever?

Dig deeper

Find out:
- more about forces that act on aeroplanes in flight
- how streamlining is related to friction.

- Objects meet resistance when they move through water as well as through air. Think of water as very thick air! Look for pictures of racing yachts and powerboats. Look at their shape. Think about the forces that make a boat move through water.

Did you know?

- Objects that travel through the air very fast get very hot on the outside because of friction.
- Rub your hands together and you can feel the heat too.
- Matches use friction to ignite.

Investigating aeroplanes

Your challenge

- Find out how air resistance acts in the opposite direction to the weight of a falling object.
- Calculate surface area.
- Make careful measurements and repeat them.
- Make and interpret a line graph.

What to do

Carry out an investigation to see whether the size of a paper aeroplane's wings affects the distance that it flies.

Make several paper aeroplanes with different-sized wings. Use paperclips to weight the aeroplanes.

Launch the aeroplanes and measure how far they fly. Repeat two or three times with each aeroplane and take an average of your results. Why is it important to do this?

I wonder whether aeroplanes behave in the same way as parachutes.

Do big paper aeroplanes fall slower than small ones?

What about the weight of the areoplane?

Or the material it's made from?

What you need

- aeroplanes with different - sized wings
- paperclips

What to check

Now try it yourselves.

- How will you keep your test fair?
- Will increasing the size of the aeroplane and its wings change more than one factor?

What did you find?

The students made several flights using aeroplanes with different-sized wings. Here are their results:

Total wing size (cm²)	Which flew the longest
112	1st
91	2nd
70	3rd
49	4th
28	5th

The students found that the aeroplanes with the biggest wings flew the furthest distance. They thought that this was because by increasing the surface area of the wings, the air resistance was increased. This slowed down the aeroplane as it moved. Do you agree?

- Use a computer program to plot your results on a graph. Can you find a line of best fit?
- Do any of your results look strange? Can you explain your results?

Can you do better?

If you did this investigation again, would you do anything differently? How good is the students' evidence? Did they change anything else when they changed the wing size?

Now predict

- Although the students calculated the wing size in cm² they only made their wings longer. Would the results be different if they changed the shape of the wing? What would happen if the surface area stayed the same but the wings were fatter and wider? Why do you think it would make a difference?

What have you learned?

- That we measure forces in newtons (N).
- That forces act in pairs.
- That several forces may act on an object at the same time.
- When an object is stationary or moving at a constant speed the forces acting on it are balanced.
- You know that you need energy to move something.
- That if an object is moving it will carry on moving unless a force acts on it.
- That gravity is a force that pulls everything to the centre of the Earth.
- We represent forces with arrows to show their size and direction.
- That friction is a force that slows things down and can make them stop altogether.
- That air resistance and water resistance are kinds of friction.
- That when an object falls air resistance acts in the opposite direction to the weight.
- That water provides an upthrust on objects submerged in water, making them weigh less.

Find out more about...

- turning and spinning forces
- Leonardo da Vinci and flight.

Check-up

Why is it that some objects float in water and some sink? How could you make a brick float?

The answer!

Do you remember the question about the snapped carrier bag? Farida had put a lot of heavy things in the bag. The weight of the groceries pulling down was a greater force than the carrier bag could hold and so the handles snapped. Gravity pulled the groceries to the ground. The eggs broke because the force of them hitting the ground made them change shape and break!

Unit 7: Changing circuits

You know how to make a circuit to light a bulb. But can you make it brighter? How do you make a motor turn faster? What happens when you make changes to you circuit?

What do you know?

- A complete circuit is needed for electricity to flow and an electrical device to work.
- A switch can be used to make or break a circuit.
- Switches can be used to control electrical devices.
- Metals are good electrical conductors.
- Plastic is a good electrical insulator.
- Mains electricity can be dangerous!

Words to learn

battery	component
cell	conductor
circuit	insulator
circuit diagram	resistance
circuit symbol	variable resistor

Skills check

Can you...

- make careful observations?
- make and repeat careful measurements?
- collect evidence and see how good it is?
- notice patterns in your results?
- use your evidence to explain what you've found out?
- use your evidence to predict something you don't yet know?

Let's find out...

Lightning is a type of electricity. Sometimes it hits, or strikes, your house. When lightning strikes, it can make all the electricity in your house go off. Why does this happen?

Electrical circuits

Things to learn

- How to represent components in a circuit.
- Using circuit diagrams to construct and interpret electrical circuits.
- How the performance of components in a circuit can be changed.

Signs and symbols

Look at the care label on an item of your clothing. Do you know what the symbols mean? Symbols like these are used as a kind of code. They help us understand a lot of information without having to write words. Can you think of other signs and symbols we use in our lives?

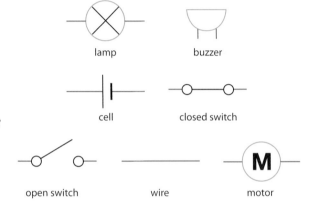

lamp

buzzer

cell

closed switch

open switch

wire

motor

Circuit symbols

Scientists working with electricity use symbols. They represent each component in a circuit. Symbols are quick to draw. People all over the world can understand them. You can construct a circuit from a circuit diagram once you know what the symbols mean. The same symbols are used by electricians and scientists all over the world.

Use the symbols to draw this circuit scientifically

All change

Changing the components in a circuit will change how the circuit works. By increasing the number of batteries, you can make bulbs brighter and motors go faster. By adding switches, you can turn circuits on and off.

Things to do

Draw a circuit

- Draw a circuit diagram.
- Challenge a friend to construct a circuit using the diagram you have drawn. How quickly can they do it?
- Are all the components in the right place? Now swap roles. How many different circuits can you make and draw? Do all of them work?

How bright?

Which of these circuits would have the brightest bulb? Why?

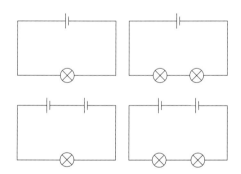

- Test your prediction.
- Draw a circuit that would be brighter than any of these.

I wonder...

What is a 'short circuit' and why can it be dangerous?

Changing components

Bulbs aren't the only components you can have in a circuit. Motors and buzzers can also be put in them.

- What happens if you move the same component into a circuit?
- What about adding different components?
- How does the number of batteries affect each of these components?

Dig deeper

Find out:
- more about circuit symbols and the other components you can have in a circuit.

Did you know?

- Circuit symbols are international. Any electrician anywhere can read them.
- Main electricity can be very dangerous. It can kill you. It can travel through your body and through water. Never touch electrical things with wet hands!

Your challenge

- Find out how the length of the wire in a circuit affects the brightness of the bulb.
- Make careful measurements and observations.

> Metal conducts electricity. Does the wire always have to be the same length?

> We could test it with bulbs and change the length of the wire to see.

> But does the wire always have to be copper?

> This wire doesn't have plastic coating so we can't use that, can we?

What to do

A circuit is made of components and wires. The wires are made of metal, such as copper. Why?

The students investigated how the length of wire affected the brightness of bulb in a circuit. They used thin fuse wire mounted between two screws on a long piece of wood. They marked the wood at 10 cm intervals and used crocodile clips to join the wire into their circuit.

The first observation they made was of the bulb in the circuit without any wire in it. Why did they do that?

What to check

Now try it yourselves.

- How will you keep the test fair? How will you judge the brightness of the bulb?
- How many readings should you take?
- How will you make sure that your components are matched?

What you need

- **fuse** wire
- metre rule
- batteries
- bulb
- connecting wire
- computer with light sensor

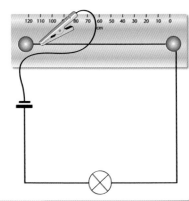

What did you find?

The students used two batteries in their circuit. They moved the crocodile clips along the wire at regular intervals to increase the length of wire in the circuit. As they did this, they noticed changes in the brightness of their bulb.

- The students decided that the longer the wire, the dimmer the bulb. Do you agree with their result?
- Can you explain what is happening to the electricity in the circuit? Why does the bulb get dimmer?

That's interesting. So the longer the wire the dimmer the bulbs.

Hang on! There are hundreds of metres of wiring in this school. Why don't we have some light bulbs that are brighter than others?

Length of fusewire in circuit (cm	Brightness of bulb
0	extremely bright
10	very bright
20	bright
30	bright
40	fairly dim
50	dim
60	cannot see any light

Now predict

- Hassan told his mum what he did in school. He wants to draw some diagrams to help him to explain. What should he draw?

Can you do better?

How could you improve on this investigation?
Would the results be the same if you used a different thickness of wire?
Is there a better way of judging the brightness of the bulb?

Exploring conductivity

Changing a plug

The electrician was putting a new plug on the television cable. He turned off the socket and removed the plug from it. He opened the plug and removed the cable. There were three wires inside the cable. First he stripped the plastic from the ends of the three wires. Then he opened the new plastic plug. He screwed each metal wire to a metal pin inside the plug. Then he put the plug together.

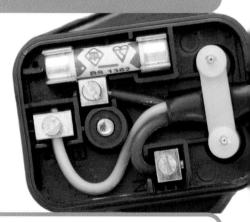

Plugs and sockets are partly made from plastic. Why?

Electricity flow

Electricity is made of tiny particles, too small to be seen, called electrons. These flow along the wires. This flow is called the electrical current.

You are a poor conductor

Your body is not a good conductor of electricity. But if the electricity is powerful enough, it will pass through you. If you are wet from the shower or the swimming pool, your body can conduct electricity. Water conducts electricity. Mains electricity can hurt or even kill you. This is why you should never turn on a light switch if you are standing in water or have wet hands.

Things to do

Conductors and insulators

Using a simple circuit, test a number of different materials to see if they are conductors or insulators.

- What do you notice?
- What general rule can you make from your observations?
- Are there any exceptions to your rule?
- Did you find more conductors or insulators?
- Why are cables made with plastic covers and metals inside?

Protection

Insulators protect us from mains electricity. But there is another protection against accidents. Mains circuits contain fuses or circuit breakers. Make a simple circuit with three wires, two with crocodile clips on, one bulb and one battery. Touching the crocodile clips together completes the circuit. Take a strand of thin metal wire wool, and hold it with one crocodile clip over a metal tray. Touch the end with the other clip to complete the circuit.

- What happens?
- How do fuses or circuit breakers cut the electricity?

Don't touch the metal part of the crocodile clip

I wonder...

Does water conduct battery electricity? What would happen if you put salt in the water?

Fuses have a thin wire inside that will burn out to prevent an accident

Dig deeper

Find out:
- more about the mains supply to your house
- more about electricity generators.

Did you know?

- Because there was no way of measuring electricity 300 years ago, scientists observed how far it went along a row of people holding hands!

Electrical resistance

Things to learn

- Resistance is how easily electricity passes through materials in a circuit.
- Different materials have different levels of resistance.
- You can change the resistance in a circuit.

Resistance

Good electrical conductors allow electricity to pass through them quite easily. We say they have low electrical resistance. Other materials have high resistance. They are insulators. Materials like plastic and rubber have high electrical resistance.

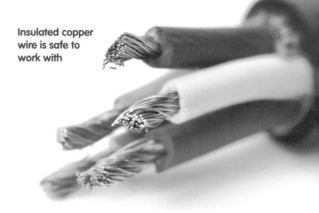

Insulated copper wire is safe to work with

More means less

Electric current is the flow of electrons. The size of the current in a circuit depends on the components in it. Each component has a resistance. They all slow the flow of electricity down slightly. Some components do this more than others. The greater the resistance, the less easily electrical current flows through the circuit.

Adding components in a circuit will increase the resistance in the circuit; bulbs will become dimmer as more of them are added. Motors will become slower. Buzzers will become quieter.

Which wire?

Copper wires are used in houses. Copper has a low electrical resistance and allows electrical current to flow through it easily. Nichrome wire has a much greater resistance. It doesn't allow electricity to pass through it easily. Because copper wire allows electricity to flow easily it is used to carry electricity long distances. The electricity will still flow. Long nichrome wires would resist current flow. Thick wires have less resistance than thin ones. Electricity can move through them move easily.

Describe the wire that would produce the brightest bulb.

Things to do

Varying the resistance

Sometimes we want to vary the resistance in a circuit deliberately. We use a variable resistor to do this. For example, we use dimmer switches to turn down lights or ceiling fans. Turning the control of the variable resistor changes the resistance in the circuit. This changes how the electrical current flows and which then alters how bright a bulb is, or how fast a fan turns.

- Make your own variable resistor. Connect the graphite lead from a pencil into your circuit. Graphite has a higher electrical resistance than the copper wires in your circuit. You can change the resistance by changing the length of graphite you use.

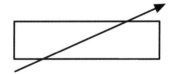

The electrical symbol for a variable resistor

I wonder...

Which materials have the greatest resistance?

A Baghdad battery

Dig deeper

Find out:
- more about resistance and changing circuits
- more about the Baghdad batteries.

Did you know?

- The filament of a light bulb is made from tungsten which glows without burning when electricity passes through it.
- Baghdad batteries generated electricity over 2500 years ago.

What have you learned?

- We use symbols to represent components in a circuit.
- Circuit diagrams are used to construct and interpret electrical circuits.
- Metals are good conductors of electricity. Plastics are good insulators and protect us from mains electricity.
- How the performance of components in a circuit can be changed.
- The length and thickness of the wire in a circuit affects the performance of components in the circuit.
- Resistance is how easily electricity passes through materials in a circuit.
- Different materials have different levels of resistance.
- How you can change the resistance in a circuit.
- How a fuse works.

Find out more about...

- the electricity of the future
- the Pharos lighthouse of Egypt.

Check-up

Kemal got an electric racing car set for his birthday. He can control the speed of the cars by squeezing the trigger on the control unit. What do you think is happening to the current in the circuit? How does the speed controller work?

The answer!

Do you remember the question about why your lights go off if your house is hit by lightning? Lightning is very powerful electricity. A battery in your circuit is normally about 1.5 V (volts). A lightning bolt is about a million volts. Too much electricity in a circuit will 'blow' the battery. This means that the wires will melt. If this happened in your house you would have to replace all the wires. Most circuits in houses are protected by fuses. They will melt or 'trip' with too much electricity, so you will not need to replace all the wires in your house.

Unit 8: Enquiry in context

Scientists use many different skills. They make predictions about what they think will happen. Scientists try out their ideas. They communicate them to other people. This might be as a sentence, a graph or a table, or even a picture. The scientists then explain what they found out and why they think it happened. What do you think they do next? Is it all over?

What do you know?

- Habitats differ.
- Different plants and animals grow in different habitats.
- Plants and animals are adapted to their environment.
- A full circuit is needed for electricity to flow.
- Some materials conduct electricity easily.
- A switch can be used to control the flow of electricity in a circuit.
- How to plan and carry out an investigation.

Words to learn

adaptation
annotate
burglar alarm
complete circuit
conductor

data
insulator
sample
switch
trend

Skills check

Can you...
- make careful observations and measurements?
- collect evidence and see how good it is?
- use your evidence to explain what you've found out?
- use your evidence to predict something you don't yet know?

Let's find out...

'Look at all the caterpillars under these leaves,' said Aunt Layla to the children. 'They are all lined up – and all munching away. Why aren't there caterpillars on top of the leaves?' asked Aunt Layla.

'There are,' said Omar. 'But there aren't as many.' 'How do you know?' said his sister. 'Because I've looked,' said Omar. 'Have you looked at all the leaves on the tree?' asked Aunt Layla. 'Of course not,' said Omar. 'Just how many leaves should we look at?'

Common cars

Anya and Riya were arguing. 'There are more silver cars in the city than any other colour,' said Anya. 'No,' said Riya. 'Blue cars are the commonest.' 'Let's find out,' said Anya. 'We can't count them all,' said Riya. 'We need a sample.' 'Let's count the cars passing the school,' said Anya. 'We shall count them at different times of day,' said Riya. 'Then we shall have a good sample.'

What to do

Anya and Riya counted cars for five minutes. They did this at four different times of the day.
They decided to count just red, black, silver and blue cars. They each had two colours to count.

What you need

- a clock
- a clipboard to record your results.

What to check

You need to be able to watch cars from a safe place. Decide how long you will count cars for.

- What colour cars will you count?
- What times of day will you choose?
- Record the results. Are there any patterns?
- What is the commonest colour?

Anya and Riya recorded their results in a table.

Time of day	Red	Black	Silver	Blue
9 a.m.	6	6	1	9
11 a.m.	4	7	2	3
1 p.m.	3	10	2	3
3 p.m.	7	5	3	10

Add up the totals. Which girl was right? Or were they both wrong? Was their sample big enough? How could they get better results?

Can you use your results?

Can you say how many cars of different colours there are in your city? Is your sample big enough?

Can you do better?

The girls stood for five minutes to count the cars. Was this long enough?

Should the girls have looked for other colours of cars as well? Why?

Now predict

● Students at another school carried out a car survey too. They counted the number of people in each car. What do you think they noticed?

Burglar alarms

Your challenge

- Plan a burglar alarm using your knowledge of science.
- Test your design.
- Improve your design so that it works better.
- Explain how your design works.
- Evaluate your design, and other people's.

What to do

Yasmin was reading a book about burglars. 'Protect your door with a pressure switch,' it said. Pressure switches work when two conductors are brought together to complete a circuit. They are separated by a squashy insulating material like sponge. Holes in the sponge should allow the two conductors to make contact. 'I'll make one of those!' thought Yasmin. 'I'll use cooking foil for the conductors. But what's best for the insulator?'

'Maybe I could use carpet,' she thought. 'Or thin rubber. Or foam. As long as the conductors can touch, it will make a switch. I'll have to wire it into a circuit.'

What else will Yasmin need to make a complete circuit? What will the switch operate? A bulb – or a buzzer?

What you need

- cooking foil
- a thin squashy insulator
- several wires
- a bulb in a bulb-holder or a buzzer
- a battery

What to check

Now try it yourselves.

- Will the circuit be complete when a burglar treads on it?
- You need to make holes in the insulator. But how many holes? Where? Why?

What did you find?

Yasmin's pressure switch only worked when really heavy people trod on it. She decided to write a complete evaluation. Her evaluation looked like this:

My pressure switch

GOOD POINTS

It's quite small. It will fit under a doormat.

It's got good connections.

It's quite nice to look at. I've decorated it.

BAD POINTS

It only works with heavy burglars.

My battery is old. It's nearly flat.

IMPROVEMENTS

I need to get a thinner insulator, or make more holes.

I need a new battery.

Can you do better?

Yasmin told people about her burglar alarm. 'How does it work?' they asked.

Yasmin should have drawn a circuit drawing of the burglar alarm. She should have drawn a diagram of the pressure switch. She could have labelled it.

- Draw a diagram of your pressure switch.
- Make notes about how it works.
- Write an evaluation of your switch.

Now predict

- Yasmin couldn't find a thin enough insulator so she took it out altogether. What happened to the switch?

Thinking like a scientist

Things to learn

- Understand the question you are answering.
- Make the right observations and measurements.
- Understand the data you have collected.
- Use scientific words correctly.
- Have ideas of how to improve your work.

Asking questions

Science is about asking questions and finding the answers. Scientists ask questions all the time. Asking the question is the hard part. You need imagination to do this.

Use your imagination. Look around you. What questions can you ask? Is it a 'How does something work?' question? Is it a 'What happens if?' question? It might even be a question about whether something is right or not!

Alhazen asked questions and established scientific methods as we know them today

The skills you use

Once you have your question, you have to find the answer. You need to test, observe and measure. There are different ways of doing this. You made a survey. You tested and observed in the burglar alarm exploration.

Other ways are fair test investigations or researching and using secondary sources to find the answer.

You use other skills too. You need to **present** your evidence. You need to **explain** what you found out. You also need to **evaluate** your evidence and say if it is good enough. You need to be able to check if your evidence supports your original prediction.

Observation

- Observation is very important. Try to notice small details. Take a walk outside. Look carefully at all the plants leaves. Collect as many different shades of green as you can.
- Arrange them in shade order. Compare them with your friend's collection. Who has the widest range? Who has the most different shades?
- Find a flower outside. Draw it in detail. Use a hand lens to notice tiny details. Try drawing an insect too.

Look at the different parts of this sunflower. What can you observe?

I wonder...

How do modern scientists share the results of their investigations.

Research

Being able to find things out by researching is a skill. It is used in many subjects. There are some tips here to help you:

- Decide on the main idea you want to find out about.
- Have some key questions you want to answer.
- List some key words you can use to help you search.
- Don't copy other people's ideas. Read them, then write them in your own words.
- Say where you found out the information.

Use these tips to find out more about one of these famous scientists:

Galileo Galilei – key words are: Sun, telescope, Earth.

Alhazen – key words are: astronomy, planets, geocentric.

Did you know?

- Scientists learn from the resuts of their investigations.
- They use these results to plan new investigations.

What have you learned?

- How to answer a scientific question.
- What evidence to collect.
- How to handle your data correctly.
- Explaining your results from what you know of science.
- Deciding just how good your evidence is.
- Planning a burglar alarm using your knowledge of science.
- Testing your design.
- Improving your design so that it works better.
- Explaining how your design works.
- Evaluating your design, and other people's.

Find out more about ...

- What happens when electricity flows.
- Stephen Hawking and his ideas about the universe.
- Ahmed Zewail and why he won the first Arabian Nobel Prize.

Check-up

'Everybody's got a bike except me!' said Akio. 'Who's everybody?' asked his mum. 'Hiro and Taro,' said Akio. 'They're not everybody,' said his mum.

Was she right? What has this got to do with sample size? What must Akio do to prove that everybody else has a bike?

The answer!

Remember the first question about how many leaves to look at? 'Enough!' is the answer. One leaf isn't enough – but a whole tree is more than Omar could manage. He and his sister need to decide on a sensible sample size. Twenty leaves, perhaps – or fifty?

Unit 1: Interdependence and adaptation checklist

What do you know?
● Think about these statements.
● Which do you know? Which can you do?

● I have learned to recognize some animals in a habitat.
● I can observe some living organisms.
● I know that animals need food to survive.
● I know that mice are found in fields and seaweed is found in the sea.
● I have learned to measure the amount a plant grows.
● I have learned to use a key to identify plants and animals.
● I can write a simple food chain to show eating patterns.
● I know that a food chain pictures how energy flows in a habitat.
● I know that food chains usually begin with a producer – a green plant.
● I know a predator eats other animals.
● I know that some plants grow tall in a rainforest to survive.
● If we don't protect the environment it will be damaged.
● I know some of the ways in which we can protect the environment.
● I can plot my data into a line graph and explain which conditions the plant grew best in.
● I can tell you if the evidence supports my predictions.

Unit 2: Scientists checklist

What do you know?
- Think about these statements.
- Which do you know? Which can you do?

- I can tell you something about what scientists do.
- I can name some famous scientists.
- I can describe some scientific discoveries.
- I can tell you something about the lives of some famous scientists.
- I can explain how they used their imagination in thinking about how the world worked.
- I have learned to work in an organized and scientific way.
- I can tell you if my evidence supports my predictions.

Unit 3: Humans checklist

What do you know?
- Think about these statements.
- Which do you know? Which can you do?

- I can name and describe the main human body systems.
- I know that I cannot live without these systems.
- I know that my organs work together.
- I can show you their positions by pointing to my body.
- I can make a picture of the main body organs.
- I can explain, using scientific terms, the circulation of the blood, the role of the lungs, what happens to food in the digestive system.
- I have learned to draw a labelled diagram of one or more of these systems.
- I know that scientists use observations to find out things.

Unit 4: More about dissolving checklist

What do you know?
- Think about these statements.
- Which do you know? Which can you do?

- I have learned to identify a range of materials, like water, wood and air.
- I have learned to use a stopwatch.
- I know that some solids dissolve.
- I know how to separate a liquid from a solid.
- I have learned to measure the volume of a liquid.
- I know how to filter a solid from a liquid.
- I know how to evaporate a liquid from a solution to leave the solid.
- I have learned to separate salt and water, or produce clean water from a muddy puddle.
- I know that rain is part of the water cycle.
- I know when to repeat my observations and measurements.
- I have learned to plot a bar chart of my results.
- I can explain why I should repeat measurements and observations.
- I have learned to put my results in a table.
- I have learned to plot a line graph of my results.

Unit 5: Reversible and irreversible changes checklist

What do you know?

- Think about these statements.
- Which do you know? Which can you do?

- I know the properties of solids, liquids and gases.
- I have learned to sort solids, liquids and gases and tell you the reasons for my classification.
- I can tell you what I observe when I watch a candle burning.
- I can explain to you what happens when materials burn.
- I can tell you why burning is not a reversible change.
- I have learned to describe the products of burning.
- I can make general statements about my observations.
- I can explain my observations.
- I can explain how solids, liquids and gases are different.
- I can explain how evaporation and condensation affect some waste products during burning.
- I have learned to select the equipment I need and use it effectively.
- I can suggest ways of improving my work.
- I can suggest why repeating an enquiry gives more reliable results.
- I have learned to draw conclusions that match my evidence.
- I can explain how some famous scientists used enquiry skills.
- I can say if my evidence supports my predictions.

Unit 6: Forces in action checklist

What do you know?
- Think about these statements.
- What do you know? Which can you do?

- I have learned to make observations of the way things move.
- I know that we need energy to move something.
- I know that a moving thing will carry on moving unless something stops it.
- I have learned to describe the effects of friction and gravity on something I am trying to move.
- I have learned to compare the differences in test results between two or more falling objects.
- I have learned to predict accurately whether something will sink or float.
- I have learned to compare differences in frictional forces, for example, how something moves over different surfaces.
- I can explain how different conditions lead to different frictional effects.
- I have learned to make changes to falling or floating objects and predict what the outcome is likely to be.
- I have learned to choose the right forcemeter for a task and make accurate forcemeter readings.
- I can explain my scientific enquiry results.
- I can make a general statement.
- I have learned to use arrows correctly to record the direction and size of forces.
- I can explain how gravity works to draw things together, and how the gravity of the Earth results in things falling towards it.
- I can explain why things weigh less in water, making use of ideas about upthrust.
- I can tell you about real examples of the use of gravity and floating.

What do you know?
- Think about these statements.
- Which do you know? Which can you do?

- I can show you how to make a simple circuit, either by talking to you or by drawing a picture.
- I have learned to make a simple circuit and explain what I have done.
- I have learned to use electrical components to make simple circuits and tell you whether my predictions about them were correct.
- I can compare the way that bulbs work in different electrical circuits.
- I have learned to carry out a fair test of insulators and conductors, or of changes in an electrical circuit, and suggest ways of doing it better.
- I know that metals are good conductors.
- I know why metal is used for electrical wires, and why it is covered in plastic.
- I can explain the reason why a bulb does not light if there is a break in the circuit or the switch is open.
- I have learned to choose components to add to my circuits, predict what they will do, and explain what happened when I added them.
- I can tell you how to put a buzzer or motor into an electric circuit, and how to control it with a switch.
- I have learned to use symbols correctly to represent my circuit.
- I have learned to make a circuit from a diagram of conventional symbols.
- I know how altering the current in my circuit can affect the brightness of bulbs.
- I can explain why the brightness of the bulbs varies.

What do you know?

● Think about these statements.
● Which do you know? Which can you do?

○ I have learned how to use a sample to give results.
○ I can describe differences in electrical circuits.
○ I have learned to plan a burglar alarm with help.
○ I have learned to link cause and effect, e.g. 'standing on my pressure pad completes the circuit'.
○ I can explain how my burglar alarm circuit works.
○ I have learned to make general statements about my enquiries.
○ I can explain my observations.
○ I have learned to select the equipment I need and use it effectively.
○ I can suggest ways of improving my work.
○ I can suggest why repeating an enquiry gives more reliable results.
○ I have learned to draw conclusions that match my evidence.
○ I can explain how some famous scientists used enquiry skills.
○ I can say if my evidence supports my predictions.

Glossary

abdomen – the lower part of your trunk – your 'tummy'

air – the gas that is all around us

alveoli – small bags, shaped like grapes, where gases are exchanged in your lungs

anchor – holding in place to stop from floating away

anus – the end of your digestive system, where solid waste leaves your body

breathe – move gases in and out of your lungs

burnt – changed completely and irreversibly by fire

camouflage – the way an animal blends with its surroundings

carnivore – any animal that eats meat

chemical reaction – when two or more chemicals come together to make a change and produce new substances

conductor – electricity travels easily through an electrical conductor

consumer – an animal in a food chain

control – unchanged part of a science investigation

crystallization – a solid becoming a regular, flat-sided shape

decant – to pour off a liquid slowly leaving the undissolved solid behind

decay – to rot

descend – to travel down

diaphragm – a muscular sheet that tightens to inflate your lungs

dimmer switch – alters the brightness of light by variable resistance

energy – the ability to do something

environment – the place that surrounds us

eyesight – the ability to see

extinct – to no longer exist

filter – to separate a solid from a liquid or gas by sieving it out

food chain – how energy flows through living things in a habitat

fuse – a thin wire in a circuit that burns out easily

glide – to move with a smooth continuous motion

gram – a metric unit of mass – one-thousandth of a kilogram

gravity – the pull of any object on another

gut – another name for your digestive system or intestine

herbivore – any animal that eats only plants

impact – the powerful effect something has on something

indigestion powder – medicine to treat difficulty in digesting food

insoluble – will not dissolve in a liquid

insulator – electricity travels poorly through an electrical insulator

intestine – the tube that digests and absorbs your food

kilogram – a metric unit of mass – one thousand grams

kinetic – a moving object has kinetic energy

lubricating oil – oil that reduces friction between surfaces

mass – the amount of stuff in something

mucus – slime that lubricates and protects

newton – the unit of measurement of force

oesophagus – the tube from your mouth to your stomach (also 'esophagus')

omnivore – an animal that eats both plants and meat

organism – any living thing, including plants and animals, as well as viruses, bacteria, fungi, moulds etc.

parachutist – person who flies a parachute

parasite – plant or animal that lives off another

permanent – cannot be reversed

pesticide – a chemical used to kill pests, especially insects

photosynthesis – how green plants trap light energy and use it to make food

plaster of Paris – a white powder made from gypsum and mixed with water to make casts and moulds

predator – an animal that eats other animals

prey – an animal that is eaten by other animals

producer – in a food chain, almost always a green plant

pulse – pressure waves of blood as your heart beats

reduce, reuse, recycle, rethink, recover – looking after our environment by becoming more responsible for what we buy, how much and how often and what we do with our waste

respiration – the exchange of gases in your lungs and the release of energy in your cells

rock pool – saltwater pond left behind by the tide

rotor – spinning wing or propeller

sample size – the selection you make when you can't count everything

saturated – a solution so full it can't dissolve any more solid

sieving – separating with a mesh that lets some objects through, but not others

sludge – thick greasy residue

soluble – will dissolve or spread all through a liquid

solute – a solid dissolved in a liquid

solvent – the liquid a solid dissolves in

soot – a black material that rises in smoke

starch – a sugar stored by a plant

stomach – the muscular bag where digestion begins

suspension – tiny pieces of a solid spread undissolved through a liquid

teeth – hard, bony, enamelled structures for biting and chewing (plural of 'tooth')

temporary – can be reversed

trachea – tough, muscular tube leading to your lungs

trend – a pattern of results showing a general direction or tendency

trial – test

tropical rainforest – dense, hot, wet forest near the equator

upthrust – the upward push of water that helps boats float

velocity – the speed of something in one direction

waterlogged – saturated with water

weight – the force of gravity on an object, depending on its mass

wick – a thread that feeds the candle flame with fuel

Index